Anatomy of a
Mentoring Program
for New Special Education
Teachers

*Christine Mason and
Marlene White*

Council for
**Exceptional
Children**
The voice and vision of special education

Council for
Exceptional
Children
The voice and vision of special education

Anatomy of a Mentoring Program for New Special Education Teachers, First edition, 2007
ISBN 0-86586-433-0
Stock No. P5837

Copyright © 2007

Council for Exceptional Children
1110 North Glebe Road, Suite 300
Arlington, Virginia 22201-5704

Table of

Contents

Table of
Contents

■ Acknowledgments

Our thanks are extended to several individuals and school districts for either participating in our pilot project or sharing their knowledge and expertise. First, our thanks to all the teachers at each of our pilot sites and their site coordinators: Randy Schelble and the Granite School District (Utah); Cathy Mellor, Francine Mayfield, and the Clark County School District (Nevada); Ellen McWilliams, Barbara Jones, and the Akron School District (Ohio); Laura Beene, Mary Smith; and the Baldwin County School District (Alabama); Sara Snyder and the Fulton County School District (Georgia); Kathy Balkman and the Henderson State University (Arkansas); Gary Smith and the Little Rock School District (Arkansas); and Betty Epanchin (University of South Florida) and the Pasco County School District (Florida). Other districts also provided valuable information, including Fairfax County (Virginia), Great Falls (Montana), and Alexandria (Virginia).

We also are grateful to:

- Our Advisory Committee members and Consensus Development Group members who assisted with the conceptual design for this project. They brought a wealth of experience from both general and special education and helped the project to proceed down the right path. They included Ms. Ismat Abdal-Haqq, Ms. Susan Bailey-Anderson, Dr. Bonnie Billingsley, Dr. Lynn Boyer, Dr. Patricia Cegelka, Dr. Lynne Cook, Ms. Pat Guthrie, Dr. David James, Dr. Clayton Keller, Dr. Elizabeth Kozleski, Ms. Ginny Love, Dr. Jonathan McIntire, Ms. Debbie Metcalf, Dr. Timothy Miller, Ms. Randy Schelble, Dr. Joseph Stowitschek, Dr. Cindy Terry, Dr. Carol Valdivieso, Dr. Ellen Williams, and Dr. Diana Wolff.

- Our external evaluator, Dr. Larry Irvin, and our research consultant, Sandra Warren.

- Several CEC staff members who provided recommendations and assisted with dissemination activities. Thanks to Richard Mainzer, Bruce Ramirez, Lynn Boyer, Phoebe Gillespie, Margie Crutchfield, and Brad Allison.

- The Mentoring Induction Project administrative assistant, Brent Mayes, who helped with the development of forms and surveys used in the project. Thanks also to the research assistants who helped with data collection, coding, interpretation, and analysis: Rikki Jamalia, Alice Richard, and Tom Phillips.

- The following individuals who assisted in the preparation, editing, refinement, review, and permission process: Sarah Priestman, Jessa Foor, Sandra Warren, Janice DeCoste, Lisa Adams, Rhonda Shepard, Ray Orkwis, and Jane Burnette. Many thanks to all of you for your time and effort.

- Thanks to the following distinguished individuals who reviewed the final manuscript: Mark Goor, Betty Epanchin, Mary Stansfield, Karen Voytecki, Susan Whitaker, Lynn Boyer, Clayton Keller, Barbara Jones, Cathy Mellor, Susan D'Aniello, and Bonnie Billingsley.

- The several publishers who gave us permission to reprint figures, tables, or selected text from their publications.

- And finally, Dr. Helen Thornton, our project officer at the U. S. Department of Education, who provided encouragement and opened doors to facilitate many activities.

Funded under award numbers H32N990047 and H325N00072, Office of Special Education Programs, U. S. Department of Education. The contents do not necessarily reflect the views or policy of OSEP, the Department of Education, any other agency of the U. S. Government, or of The Council for Exceptional Children.

■ Chapter One

Mentoring: A Lifeline for New Teachers

Learn About...

■ **Mentoring: Addressing Issues and Challenges**

■ **Aiding Teacher Retention**

■ **State Offerings**

■ **Varying Perceptions**

■ **The Mentoring Promise**

■ **Reducing Stress**

■ **The Mentoring Induction Project**

Effective mentoring programs benefit all teachers. However, research shows that new teachers particularly benefit from mentoring programs. New teachers who become involved in a mentoring program have shown an increase in self-confidence, improved collaboration skills, further use of research-based strategies, and an enhanced ability to effectively differentiate their instructional practices. Mentoring also enhances the professional development and revitalization of experienced teachers, who indicate that it has increased their teaching effectiveness (Billingsley, 1993; Boyer, 1999; Colbert & Wolff, 1992; Evertson & Smithey, 2000; King-Sears, 1995; Lane & Canosa, 1995; White & Mason, 2002). As the awareness about the benefit of teacher mentoring programs increases, so do the number of mentoring programs nationwide.

This book provides an orientation to mentoring programs and a detailed look at the essential functions that make up the anatomy of a mentoring program. Research suggests that four areas are crucial to a mentoring program's success (Feiman-Nemser & Parker, 1993; Griffin et al., 2003; Whitaker, 2000). They are:

- Formal expectations of the mentoring program.
- Roles and responsibilities of the mentoring team.
- Mentor teacher selection procedures.
- Orientation and training for the mentoring team.

This book incorporates research on mentoring and provides examples from the Mentoring Induction Project, a national study of mentoring implementation. In separate chapters, it discusses each of the organs and bodily systems that make up a healthy and successful mentoring program:

- Skeleton of program design.

- Heart of the program: New teachers.

- Central nervous system: Mentor teachers.

- Circulatory system: Mentoring program coordinators.

- Respiratory system: Building administrators.

How to Use this Manual

This manual is designed for mentors, new teachers, coordinators of mentoring programs, and principals who want to make a difference for students in special education. Both special educators and general educators—particularly those who are coordinating mentor programs—should find useful material to inform their decision making and implementation of mentoring programs.

Although each chapter is written for a particular audience—new teachers, mentors, mentor coordinators, building administrators—readers will find useful information in all chapters. For example, principals will find that the main points they need to focus on are contained in Chapter 6, yet there are many ideas in the other chapters that they can use to enhance the mentoring program. Similarly, mentors will gain practical ideas for helping new teachers in Chapter 3, supporting the entire mentoring program in Chapter 5, and capitalizing on the support of building administrators in Chapter 6.

■ *Mentoring—Addressing the Issues*

The growth of mentoring programs is fueled by a number of issues that face educational systems nationwide. The most critical are teacher shortages and teacher retention. Schools also face challenges brought by new legislation affecting teacher qualifications. While mentoring can address these issues, and more states are offering mentoring programs, perceptions of mentoring programs vary. Clear guidelines and systematic planning is crucial to the success of mentoring programs.

Today, serious teacher shortages exist in four primary areas (science, math, special education, and English as a Second Language). These shortages have resulted in an increased national effort not only to attract but also to keep teachers in these fields.

According to a report in *Education Week* (2004), the U. S. Department of Education estimates that colleges and universities are projected to be able to supply only about 50 percent of the 200,000 new special education teachers that will be needed during the next five years. At the beginning of the 21st century, 98 percent of all school districts in America reported a shortage of special education teachers (American Association for Employment in Education, 1999). The increased number of uncertified teachers who are hired every year serves as another indicator of the severity of the shortage of special education teachers. During the 2000-2001 school year alone, about 47,0000 special education positions were filled by uncertified teachers, a 23 percent increase from the previous year (Center on Personnel Studies in Special Education, 2004).

There is an alarmingly high attrition of special education teachers. Approximately 6 percent of special education teachers leave classrooms each year (Boe, Barkanic, & Loew, 1999), and another 7.4 percent of special education teachers transfer to general education (Boe, Bobbitt, Cook, & Barkanic, 1998), resulting in an attrition rate of more than 13 percent per year. While the reasons for this national shortage are numerous, most troubling is the high attrition rate. This is especially troubling given the effort that teachers have taken to become certified in special education, the efforts the districts have taken to hire certified teachers, and the knowledge that these teachers have gained both through their coursework and their in-class experience. High attrition rates contribute to a lack of direction and instability in program implementation. High attrition rates also often translate to lower student achievement as new hires need to acclimate to the culture and expectations of the school as well as learning instructional strategies.

■ *Mentoring—Addressing Challenges Related to Educating Students with Disabilities*

Special education today is in a state of flux as school districts throughout the nation struggle to find ways to keep students with special needs in inclusive environments and meet the achievement gains expected for Annual Yearly Progress (AYP). While the *No Child Left Behind Act* of 2001 (NCLB) (P.L. 107-110) focused a spotlight on the instruction of students with Individual Education Programs (IEPs), progress for these students remains an agonizing concern, with few assurances that one instructional path will be more effective than another.

The variables of teacher shortages, the number of new teachers, and the expectations for special educators to be highly qualified through certification in subject matter areas further complicate this landscape. In providing services to students with disabilities, districts are challenged with the enormous task of ensuring that students with disabilities receive an appropriate education while simultaneously struggling to find appropriately trained teachers.

After more than a quarter of a century of implementation, first through the *Education of All Handicapped Children Act* of 1975, and then the *Individuals with Disabilities Education Improvement Act* of 2004 (IDEA 2004), many assessment and instructional practices that have evolved are being reexamined and revised. With higher expectations has come a need for results that can be demonstrated early and within a relatively short period of time.

School districts are now mandated to hire and retain teachers who meet specific conditions for being "highly qualified." According to requirements of NCLB, all teachers, including special educators, are expected to be certified in the subjects that they are teaching. This has required some clarification for special educators teaching multiple subjects and most states are addressing these personnel requirements under the High Objective Uniform State Standard of Evaluation (HOUSSE) provisions of NCLB. The HOUSSE provisions allow states to develop alternative procedures for teachers to demonstrate competence in the subjects they teach, and many states are relying on subject matter tests as a primary measure of teacher competence.

The U. S. Department of Education (2004) has provided some non-regulatory guidance on how the expectations for HOUSSE apply to special educators:

> Special education teachers who provide instruction in core academic subjects must meet the highly qualified teacher requirements for those core academic subjects that they teach. These requirements apply whether a special education teacher provides core academic instruction in a regular classroom, a resource room, or another setting (U. S. Department of Education, 2004, p. 17).

However, as indicated in that same document, if special education teachers are providing consultative services and are not the primary instructor, then they are not required to meet the NCLB requirements of being highly qualified:

> There are many activities that special education teachers may carry out that would not, by themselves, require those teachers to be highly qualified in a particular subject matter. Special educators who do not directly instruct students in any core academic subjects or who provide only consultation to highly qualified teachers of core academic subjects in adapting curricula, using behavioral supports and interventions, or selecting appropriate accommodations, do not need to demonstrate subject-matter competency in those subjects. These special educators could also assist students with study skills or organizational skills and reinforce instruction that the child has already received from a highly qualified teacher in that core academic subject (U. S. Department of Education, 2004).

As the Council of Administrators of Special Education (CASE) (2004) has pointed out, special educators should be considered highly qualified in special education if they meet the state/provincial certification requirements, which should include any required demonstration of competencies. CASE also has commented on the term "highly qualified," and in so doing, referenced the long-held expectations for highly qualified special education teachers:

> "Highly qualified" as defined by NCLB relates only to the delivery of course content instruction. However, CASE believes the unique skills of the special educator in areas of methodologies, adaptations, accommodations, modifications, and functional skills, are indicative of a status of "highly qualified" in special education. Acknowledgement of the importance of these skills as well as core content competencies should be considered in the definition of "highly qualified" for all teachers. CASE further recognizes that educational licensure is within the jurisdiction of each state and province and does not intend to impose specific standards on this certification process (Council of Administrators of Special Education, 2004, p. 1).

Mentoring helps schools meet NCLB requirements, not only by improving the skills of teachers, but also by helping to retain them.

■ *Mentoring Aids Teacher Retention*

What should districts do to meet the simultaneous need for higher academic achievement and better prepared teachers? The answers are complex and multifaceted, and mentoring for teachers by itself is not the answer. However, high-quality mentoring programs can:

- Help new teachers develop, refine, and apply their repertoire of skills.

- Support new teachers in developing the confidence to stay in education.

- Expand the capabilities of schools to implement effective educational practices.

Mentoring programs can be considered a low-cost solution because they do not require sophisticated technologies, extensive use of consultants, or dramatic increases in staffing. Instead, high-quality mentoring programs rely on trusted master teachers to share their experience; be an onsite resource; and provide support to new teachers who will inevitably experience doubts, have questions, and need guidance during their first few years of teaching.

New teachers experience a multitude of difficulties that contribute to high stress levels, lowered job satisfaction, and increased likelihood of leaving the field of education (Gersten et al., 2001). It is no easy feat to teach and manage a classroom of 20 to 30 youth—or to advise general educators about how to modify instruction for a struggling student—when first trying out their new roles. Often, new teachers must search for effective instructional and discipline strategies while attempting to be fair, firm, and consistent.

New teachers are more likely to stay in teaching and feel more confident in their ability to teach if they have informal building supports, including mentoring (Johnson & Kardos, 2002). In a study by Brownell and her colleagues (2004), beginning general educators who were teaching students with disabilities in inclusive environments reported that informal building supports—such as mentoring—helped them build their confidence, increase their self-reliance, develop a sense of efficacy, and manage their levels of stress. Similarly, CEC's Bright Futures report (Kozleski, Mainzer, & Deshler, 2001) indicated that a sense of isolation, lack of administrative support, and paperwork all contribute to job dissatisfaction among special education teachers.

New special educators may find that when collaborating with general education teachers those teachers would prefer not to be charged with making appropriate accommodations, but rather to simply leave that student's instruction to the special educator—or find a way to dismiss the student from their class. Many general educators today have their hands full facilitating the instruction of all the students in their class and simply have not learned strategies to make the more extensive modifications that may be required for students with special needs.

Effective collaboration is a difficult task for new special educators, and especially for those without previous teaching or other related experience. While a very small percentage of new special educators may transfer from general education to special education, and some may come as mid-career changers from other fields, most often special educators will enter teaching directly from their university programs. Teachers without related experience, who may very well be tentative and uncertain of their approach, will have difficulty speaking with the authority that may be necessary for effective collaboration with other teachers. The help of a nearby mentor can be extremely valuable, not only to boost confidence, but also to help the new teacher solve problems when difficulties arise.

For example, new special educators can share their plans for collaboration with their mentors. In turn, the mentors can share information on what they know about the most effective ways to collaborate with individual teachers within a particular school. Moreover, mentors can share strategies for communicating with teachers who are resisting efforts to engage in joint planning, co-teaching, or other collaborative efforts.

Some new special educators are very well prepared. However, sometimes even they find that they are not adequately prepared for a particular teaching position. A mismatch between a teacher's training and a specific job can lead to frustration, missteps, and even a sense of failure on the part of a new teacher. For example, some teachers are prepared for elementary school and then placed at the secondary level. Other teachers may be prepared to work with students with learning disabilities and then be employed to work with students with emotional problems. Some teachers are prepared for suburban environments and then are employed in rural or inner-city areas where resources may be very different, and student attitudes or the culture of the school district may be very different than the teacher's experience during student teaching or an internship. Another major concern arises from the broad subject areas that special educators are expected to cover—particularly at the secondary level where more in-depth knowledge is required (Mastropieri, 2001).

Teachers new to the profession and new to a geographic area typically need and value support and assistance

from a trusted mentor as they become acclimated to their schools and communities. These new educators need to understand the dynamics of their environment and how to contribute most effectively in that environment. Even under the best of conditions, new special education teachers appreciate the unique support and guidance a mentor can provide to help them navigate through their first year of teaching.

■ States Offering Mentoring Programs

Data gathered by the Education Commission of the States and the North Central Regional Educational Laboratory (NCREL) show that 27 states offer mentoring programs (Learning Point Associates, 2004). Of these, 22 require mentoring for new teachers, two have a policy for voluntary mentoring programs, two are piloting programs, and one requires mentoring only for teachers in alternative certification programs. While the expectations of states for mentoring programs continue to vary, there is a growing recognition that the effectiveness of mentoring is dependent upon sufficient funding, preparation of mentors, and accompanying expectations for inservice support of new teachers and involvement of administrators.

State policies on mentoring were compiled on a web site maintained by the Education Commission of the States and NCREL (Learning Point Associates, 2004). Connecticut, for example, is one of 22 states that require a formal mentoring induction program. In Connecticut, teachers complete the Portfolio Induction Program with school-based support provided by a mentor or support team. During the first year Connecticut recommends that teachers also access discipline-specific online orientation sessions. During years two and three, school-based support is optional; however, during these years, teachers are required to submit a teaching portfolio.

In comparison, Illinois expects mentors to complete a training program and not be assigned responsibility to assist more than five new teachers during any given school year. Illinois further recommends that mentors hold the same type of teaching certificate as the new teachers and also includes very specific recommendations for observations and videoconferencing or videotaping new teachers, as well as requirements for specific professional development activities and formative assessment of the professional development activities of new teachers.

While the NCREL web site has been dismantled, similar data are now located on a site dedicated to teacher quality and maintained as part of NCLB (**https:// www.teacherquality.us/Public/PromisingPractices. asp?PPCategoryID=4**).

The growth in mentoring programs has generally been attributed to concern about the attrition of new teachers and increased use of alternative certification procedures. As more teachers are hired without extensive background or training in education, mentoring has been seen as one way to increase the resources available to assist new teachers. High quality mentoring programs can help new teachers develop, refine, and apply their repertoire of skills.

There are few research data to support the efficacy of mentoring for teachers hired with emergency credentials. However, there is some recognition that mentoring programs should differ for beginning teachers, fully certified teachers, and teachers hired under alternative certification. Special education administrators have suggested that teachers hired under alternative certification routes may require more intensive and prolonged mentoring supports, including more frequent meetings with mentors, more opportunities to observe experienced classroom teachers, and additional inservice training sessions on specific topics such as development of IEPs, classroom management, and student assessment and evaluation.

The suggestions offered in this book are for mentoring programs for teachers who have completed university teacher education programs and are fully licensed. While many of the recommendations can apply to teachers who are emergency credentialed or are working toward alternative certification, these teachers will have additional needs—such as more intensive mentoring, a longer induction program, etc.

■ *Perceptions of Mentoring Programs Vary*

Despite growth in the number of mentoring programs, the perceived usefulness of these programs for special education teachers varies. In a recent study of 1,153 teachers, 60 percent of the new teachers participated in mentoring induction programs, but only about two-thirds of these teachers indicated that mentoring was helpful (Billingsley, Carlson, & Klein, 2004).

A smaller survey of teachers conducted in Oregon found that beginning teachers valued several types of supports, including both informal supports by peers and administrators and formalized mentoring programs (Oregon Recruitment and Retention Project, 2004). However, as with the larger national study reported by Billingsley et al. (2004), mentoring was not valued equally by all respondents. In the Oregon survey, 75 percent of career changers who were new special education teachers and 66 percent of other beginning special educators rated mentoring as helpful.

One reason for the questionable efficacy of mentoring for special education teachers may be the wide fluctuations in the quality, intensity, and fit between mentoring programs and the needs of special education teachers. Billingsley et al. (2004), in fact, reported that when induction programs involved higher levels of support, teachers said classes were more manageable and they were able to be effective with more difficult students.

A three-year investigation of mentoring for special educators found that the needs of special education teachers are quite specific. They include the need for assistance on topics that may or may not be covered in more general mentoring programs, such as developing IEPs (White & Mason, 2002).

■ *The Mentoring Promise*

When implemented with careful consideration of the school district expectations and needs, mentoring programs can effectively reduce the stress associated with the first year of teaching, potentially increasing new special education teachers' feelings of job satisfaction, confidence, job performance, and overall commitment to the profession. Mentoring induction programs for teachers have reduced attrition rates in some districts by nearly two-thirds (Darling-Hammond, 2000). Mentoring has helped to increase retention of beginning special educators (Odell & Ferraro, 1992; Recruiting New Teachers, 1999; Wald, 1998; Whitaker, 2000). Effective mentoring programs can help new teachers keep their passion for teaching, a driving force that can lead to feelings of reward as individual students make even small gains. This passion also can help teachers build their resilience as they learn that, even under very demanding conditions, they are committing themselves to a profession that will serve students who otherwise may be left to flounder.

We see each other...we talk daily. It's a daily thing, we're side by side. That's the best setup for a mentor/mentee because I don't have to wait until I can get a break to go and make a phone call or it's time for me to go to this school, or my mentor come to this school. I have instant access to the information that I need, and that is a big plus.

**—New Teacher,
Mentoring Induction Project**

While mentoring programs show promise for increasing teacher skills and effectiveness, recent findings (Griffin et al., 2003) suggest that mentoring will be more effective if it includes the following elements:

- Culture of shared responsibility and support.

- Interactions between new and experienced teachers.
- Continuum of professional development.
- De-emphasized focus on evaluation.
- Clear goals and purposes.
- Diversified content.

Griffin et al. (2003) also concluded from their analysis of 10 research studies on mentoring in special education that mentoring is more effective when mentors are special educators and if there is frequent contact between the mentor and the new teacher.

■ *Mentoring—Reducing Stress and Creating a Stable Workforce*

Mentoring has great promise in helping to reduce the stress associated with the first year of teaching. Effective mentoring has great benefits for both the new teacher and the mentor teacher, including:

- Increased job satisfaction.
- Increased effectiveness.
- Greater commitment to the profession.
- A more nurturing overall school climate.

As Little (1990) explains, the "mantle of mentorship purportedly creates an incentive for teacher retention and commitment by conferring public recognition and reward on the most accomplished teachers" (p. 300). In addition, mentoring programs that produce a more stable teacher work force, highlight more competent, satisfied teachers, and showcase teaching as a desirable career can attract new teachers to the field (Recruiting New Teachers, 1999).

■ *The Mentoring Induction Project*

In response to the need for a systematic, effective, and empirically based mentoring model that would be inclusive of the needs of special educators, a set of guidelines was developed by the Mentoring Induction Project at the Council for Exceptional Children (CEC). This three-year project, funded by the Office of Special Education Programs of the U.S. Department of Education (OSEP), was designed to build on existing research on mentoring in special education and general education to develop a national set of mentoring guidelines that would be particularly appropriate for mentoring special educators. The project was guided by the expertise of a Consensus Development Group and a National Advisory Committee that included some of the foremost researchers in mentoring and induction in general education and special education, as well as teachers, administrators, and policymakers.

The Mentoring Induction Guidelines (which are summarized in Chapter 2) were developed through the following steps:

- A review of the literature and discussion with researchers throughout the nation.

- A conceptual meeting with key advisors to discuss parameters, barriers, intended outcomes, sites for field testing, and evaluation components. These advisors were members of the Consensus Development Group and National Advisory Committee.

- Social validation through focus groups with beginning special education teachers, mentors, and administrators at five sites in urban and suburban school districts in various geographic regions throughout the United States.

- Review of CEC's statement on mentoring from CEC's *What Every Special Educator Must Know:*

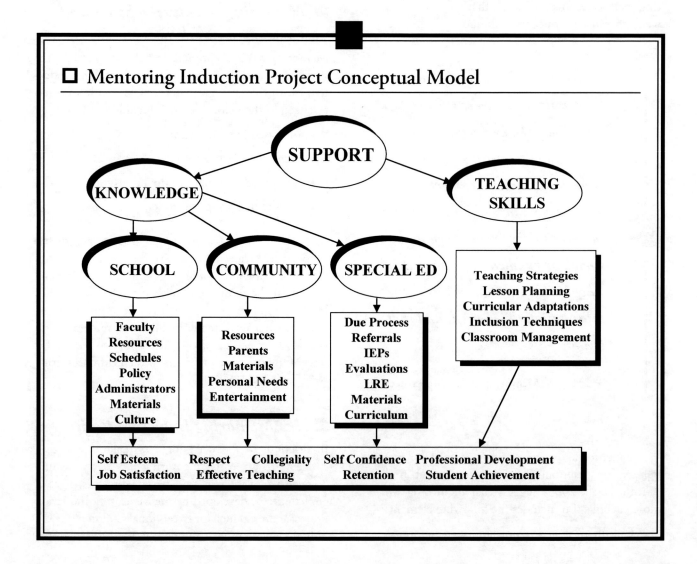

❑ Mentoring Induction Project Conceptual Model

SUPPORT

KNOWLEDGE

TEACHING SKILLS

SCHOOL   COMMUNITY   SPECIAL ED

Teaching Strategies
Lesson Planning
Curricular Adaptations
Inclusion Techniques
Classroom Management

Faculty
Resources
Schedules
Policy
Administrators
Materials
Culture

Resources
Parents
Materials
Personal Needs
Entertainment

Due Process
Referrals
IEPs
Evaluations
LRE
Materials
Curriculum

Self Esteem   Respect   Collegiality   Self Confidence   Professional Development
Job Satisfaction   Effective Teaching   Retention   Student Achievement

Ethics, Standards, and Guidelines for Special Educators (5th ed.) (2003). Input was solicited from the Teacher Education Division (TED) and CASE of CEC.

- Review of the guidelines by a cross-section of administrators, teacher educators, parents, and distinguished teachers.

- Pilot testing and refinement for two years at four sites across the United States.

- A second tier of pilot testing for 12 months in three additional sites, resulting in implementation at a total of seven national sites.

The project developed a conceptual model that outlined the philosophy on support and guidance needed for first year special educators. [For a graphic of the conceptual model, see the text box, *Mentoring Induction Project Conceptual Model.*] This model is based on

support, not evaluation, in two areas—knowledge and teaching skills. The Mentoring Induction Project Conceptual Model is based on the following assumption:

> New teachers need knowledge, general support, and assistance with teaching skills.

By increasing knowledge of the school, community, and special education and by increasing specific teaching skills (such as skills in classroom management and instruction), new teachers become more proficient and more confident.

Using this model to guide the mentoring program will help new teachers develop greater feelings of self-esteem, respect, and job satisfaction. It should result in more effective teaching, greater student achievement, and higher levels of teacher retention.

■ Chapter Two

Program Design

The Skeleton of a Mentoring System

Learn About...

■ **Formal Expectations**

■ **Essential Features**

■ **Roles And Responsibilities**

■ **Mentoring Program Structure**

A strong framework is crucial to the proper functioning of a mentoring program. Just as strong bones are integral to the skeleton, certain characteristics are essential to the strength of the mentoring program. Effective mentoring programs provide a supportive skeleton by encouraging beginning teachers to proactively request information and help, and to take advantage of scheduled trainings and professional development opportunities. These activities strengthen their ability to deal with whatever may arise in the classroom.

■ *Formal Expectations of the Mentoring Program*

The purpose of a mentoring program for special educators is to offer personal and professional support and assistance to first-year teachers and help them with the transition from being students to being teachers. Mentoring programs should be:

- Assistance-oriented.

- Designed to meet the needs of the mentoring team.

- Allocated sufficient time to perform all of the activities involved in mentoring.

Assistance-Oriented

Mentoring programs should be assistance-oriented rather than assessment-oriented. There is a distinct and fundamental difference between support and evaluation, and the two must be provided separately (Brock & Grady, 1998; Council for Exceptional Children, 1997; Feiman-Nemser & Parker, 1993; Recruiting New

Teachers, 1999; White, 1995). Moreover, when the mentoring program is tied to certification measures as its primary focus, new teachers tend to adjust their behaviors to match only those required for certification (Ganser et al., 1998; Griffin, 1985; White, 1995).

Designing the Mentoring Team

Mentoring needs to be designed to meet the needs of the mentoring team. When mentoring programs are implemented too quickly—without the purposes or framework understood by all involved, and without taking into account the goodness of fit between the model and the needs of the current personnel—participants generally do not perceive the experience to be beneficial (Ganser et al, 1998; Gold, 1996; Lawson, 1992; White, 1995). While there are a number of models for mentoring programs in different states and districts, the mentoring team may not have time to consider the pros and cons of various models for mentoring. In these cases, the onus must fall on a small, dedicated group of professionals who will be charged not only with designing the program but also with getting the buy-in and support from others within the system. For this to happen, special educators must work with those individuals who manage and implement the broader mentoring programs within their districts and states.

Mentoring Takes Time

Time, is identified as "the most highly valued and closely protected of teachers' resources" (Little, 1990, p. 309), and it is key to a successful mentoring relationship. Self-reports of 156 first year special education teachers indicate that weekly mentor/teacher contact increases program effectiveness and that unstructured, informal contacts tend to be more effective than formal meetings and observations (Whitaker, 2000). School systems that implement mentoring programs signal the importance they place on the mentor, the new teacher, and the success of the program by the amount of time they allocate for the mentor's work (Colbert & Wolff, 1992; Darling-Hammond, 1996; Ganser et al. 1998; Huling-Austin, 1992).

In considering the needs of the team, release time is one of the most critical variables. Release time must be balanced between the school day and after-school hours. The proper balance allows new teachers to observe effective teaching and management techniques during classes, but does not place a great burden on mentors' classroom time. Mentors' out-of-classroom time should not be so great that they feel their own teaching effectiveness is compromised (Little, 1990). Activities planned during release time must match the needs and sophistication of the new teacher and should include time for planning, consultation, modeling, observation, and professional development activities (Darling-Hammond, 1996; Recruiting New Teachers, 1999; Study of Personnel Needs in Special Education, 2001).

■ *Essential Features of a Mentoring Program*

Successful mentoring programs are characterized by the following features:

- **Clear objectives**. The mentoring program, including its purposes and options, must be clear and agreed upon by the beginning special education teachers, experienced mentors, representatives from the district, and building level administrators.

- **Knowledge sharing**. Information concerning roles, expectations, policies, provisions, and desired outcomes of the mentoring program are shared with and understood by beginning teachers, mentors, and administrators.

- **Adequate resources**. The mentoring program is planned and adequately funded.

- **Full participation**. All first-year special education teachers are expected to participate in the mentoring program.

- **Special education coordination**. Mentoring for special education teachers may be coordinated with other more general mentoring programs within the school district, but they must specifically address those issues unique to special education.

■ **Process-based**. The mentoring program is designed to provide assistance and support only and should not be related to any formal evaluations, certification requirements, or reemployment issues.

More detail about the essential steps to planning and implementing a mentoring program is provided in Chapter 5.

■ *Roles and Responsibilities of the Mentoring Team*

For a new teacher mentoring or induction program to be successful and effective, there must exist a culture of shared responsibility and support (Griffin et al., 2003). Working as a team involves respecting the role that each player takes, and it means helping to strengthen the skills of each team member. The philosophy that teachers' skills fall along a continuum of development acknowledges the freshness a beginning teacher brings to the classroom while respecting the achievements of the veteran or master teacher (Billingsley, 2002). Regardless of experience, all teachers can benefit from professional development opportunities that meet their specific needs and are presented in a manner that encourages participation.

The new teacher, mentor teacher, building administrator, and mentor coordinator make up the mentoring team. Each has specific roles and responsibilities that must be understood and employed. Each role is summarized here.

The Heart of a Mentoring Program: New Teachers

Effective teachers have a passion for teaching and often hold deep feelings of caring for the children they teach. These feelings are often the primary reason that individuals initially choose to enter the teaching profession. Once they begin to teach, they are faced with the day-to-day realities, responsibilities, and stresses of teaching. Like a heart in stress, new teachers can be considered to be in survival mode, often overwhelmed with all the responsibilities of teaching on a day-to-day

basis. Some know that they need help, but either don't know whom to ask for help or are hesitant to ask in fear it will make them appear less competent. Some are so overwhelmed they "don't know what they don't know" and therefore, don't even realize they need help (White & Mason, 2002). Having a nearby mentor can be a great help.

Beginning teachers must remain open and responsive to feedback and suggestions to enhance and strengthen their teaching and management skills. In the Mentoring Induction Project, every beginning teacher asked for help from his or her mentor at some point during the year on topics ranging from time management (53 percent) to special education paperwork (91 percent). The needs of new teachers are discussed in Chapter 3.

> *"My mentor teacher has been wonderful because we share a room...and we have a door between us. Anytime I need something, I just open the door...."*
>
> **—New Teacher,**
> **Mentoring Induction Project**

The Central Nervous System: Mentor Teachers

This critical central nervous system of the mentoring program—mentor teachers—guides and supports beginning teachers. Mentors encourage new teachers by reinforcing principles of action. Mentors are conduits for knowledge. They help connect new teachers to valuable resources. Their feedback helps new teachers improve their instructional skills and gain confidence.

The role of the mentor teacher must be well defined in order to avoid ambiguity and unattainable expectations (Darling-Hammond, 1996; Feiman-Nemser,

Parker, & Zeichner, 1992; Lane & Canosa, 1995; Little, 1990). The primary role of the mentor teacher is to guide, assist, and support the new teacher during that crucial first year of teaching. Experienced mentor teachers have described that role as:

- **Providing solutions**. As a provider of solutions, supplying the new teacher with strategies to improve overall teaching effectiveness.

- **Becoming a partner in problem solving**. As a partner in problem solving, mentors guide the new teacher to develop his or her own teaching style based on best practice without "encroaching on their fragile autonomy" (Feiman-Nemser & Parker, 1993, p. 699).

- **Helping new teachers navigate the system**. As a local guide, mentors help new teachers gain entry into the teaching environment.

- **Being an educational companion and coach**. As an educational companion, mentors work on long-term professional goals with the new teacher.

- **Helping new teachers change as appropriate**. As an agent of change, mentors help new teachers build networks and address the isolation associated with the first year (Feiman-Nemser, 1992; Feiman-Nemser, Parker, & Zeichner, 1992; Feiman-Nemser & Parker, 1993).

The mentor teacher should not be part of any formative evaluation and should not work to remediate the teaching skills of the new special educator. Moreover, mentor teachers cannot replace systematic, planned preparation programs. Chapter 4 provides more detail about the roles of mentors.

The Circulatory System: The Mentoring Program Coordinator

District level coordinators are needed to:

- **Plan and implement mentoring for special educators**. The coordinator takes the essential steps of planning and implementing a mentoring program. The ultimate success or failure of the mentoring program rests with the coordinator,

who is responsible for establishing and updating the mentoring program, and for communicating with all stakeholders.

- **Collaborate and communicate with all parties**. Coordinators need to consider how best to collaborate with district mentoring and induction programs for general educators, individual building principals, and nearby universities—all of which may be involved or have the desire to be involved in providing supports to mentors and new teachers.

- **Circulate information, resources, and support throughout the entire extended mentoring program system**. The coordinator establishes arteries for distributing information and requests and veins to gather information and support and bring it back to the heart—new teachers.

- **Suggest enhancements and improvements**. The coordinator usually recommends guidelines for the mentoring programs, inservice training for both mentors and new teachers, and policies regarding release time for observations, conferencing, and support meetings.

The coordinator may find that his or her base of support is strengthened by working with a team of general and special educators and other administrators in making policy and procedural recommendations. Because the impact of the mentoring program depends upon the adequacy of the supports, the coordinator's role in influencing others and building the case for mentoring is pivotal. The role of mentor coordinators in planning and implementing a mentoring program and gathering and circulating information, resources, and support for the entire team is discussed further in Chapter 5.

The Respiratory System: Building Administrators

Like oxygen, administrators provide the catalyst to energize the system. The role of the building administrator in the effectiveness and retention of special education teachers is crucial (Billingsley, 2002; Cross & Billingsley, 1994; Gersten et al. 2001; Griffin et al., 2003; Miller, Brownell, & Smith, 1999). When special education teachers perceive that the building level

administrator is supportive, they report reduced levels of stress, fewer role problems, higher levels of professional commitment, greater collegiality with other faculty, greater job satisfaction, and increased intent to stay (Cross & Billingsley, 1994; Gersten, et al., 2001; Singh & Billingsley, 1996; Westling & Whitten, 1996; White, 1995).

In effective mentoring programs, administrators:

- Participate in the selection of mentor teachers.

- Support the mentoring program.

- Provide mentor teachers and new teachers with opportunities to participate in the mentoring process.

- Participate in the mentoring program evaluation.

Administrators are responsible for ensuring that new teachers and mentors have ample opportunities to inhale fresh wisdom and knowledge through observations, consultations, and attendance at planned training sessions.

Administrators in the Mentoring Induction Project helped facilitate successful mentoring by selecting master teachers as mentors and monitoring the mentoring relationships in their buildings. New teachers and mentor teachers who participated in the Mentoring Induction Project stated that administrative support was very important for successful mentoring (M = 4.1 on 5-point Likert scale) and felt their administrators were "somewhat to very" supportive of their mentoring efforts (M = 3.6). The types of support provided by building administrators are discussed in Chapter 6.

■ *Putting These Roles Together: Overview of the Mentoring Program Structure*

The mentoring induction guidelines summarized in the following checklist were developed to be general enough so that individual school districts would have the necessary latitude to use them in ways that fit their individual needs and programs. However, the effectiveness of mentoring programs has sometimes been compromised due to inadequate oversight of the program, provisions for release time for the mentor and first year special education teacher, training for mentors, or administrative support. Therefore, these guidelines include broad recommendations as well as components targeted as essential for adequate support of beginning special education teachers. The Mentoring Induction Checklist is found in the text box. The Mentoring Induction Checklist can be used in the following ways:

- To ensure that the program includes all of the essential program features.

- To make arrangements to provide the necessary activities and supports to new special education teachers, mentor teachers, and administrators.

- To ensure that the critical features continue to be active within the mentoring program after it is operational.

While the checklist will be especially useful to Mentoring Program Coordinators, anyone involved in a mentoring induction program can use the checklist to consider the strengths and weaknesses of their school's plan and program. The checklist also can become a resource for continual program improvement.

☐ The Mentoring Induction Checklist (page 1 of 4)

Essential Features of the Mentoring Program

☐ **Collaborative development**: Clear mentoring program objectives were developed collaboratively for the district with input from administrators, new teachers, and mentors.

☐ **Awareness**: Information on roles, expectations, policies, provisions, and desired outcomes is shared and understood by all stakeholders.

☐ **Adequate resources**: Human and fiscal resources have been anticipated and budgeted.

☐ **Full participation**: All first-year special educators are expected to participate.

☐ **Coordination among programs**: Mentoring of special educators is coordinated with other mentoring programs but addresses special education concerns.

☐ **Process-based**: Relationship between mentor and new special educator is for support and guidance. The mentor has no formal evaluation responsibilities.

☐ **Responsibility**: District level person is given specific responsibilities to coordinate and oversee mentoring program.

☐ **Compensation**: Mentors receive compensation of their choice (e.g., monetary, perks, classroom materials, technology, etc.).

☐ **Evaluation**: Feedback obtained from mentoring team is used to make recommended changes.

Mentor Selection: Qualities and Characteristics of Mentor Teachers

The mentor is:

☐ A special education teacher with three to five years experience in the district.

☐ Teaching in the same school as the new teacher.

☐ Teaching the same type of student population, at the same grade level, as the new teacher.

☐ Volunteering to be a mentor.

☐ Viewed as a master teacher by the school administrator.

Orientation and Training: Beginning Special Education Teachers

☐ Beginning special education teachers hired prior to school openings participate with mentors in inservice and planning before school opens.

☐ Beginning special teachers hired after school openings are paired with mentors and provided with orientation to the program as soon as possible.

☐ Beginning special teachers have the opportunity to meet regularly with other new teachers to share materials, strategies, successes, and concerns.

☐ The Mentoring Induction Checklist (page 2 of 4)

Beginning special education teachers have access to professional development on the following topics:

❑ Behavior management techniques.

❑ IEP development and implementation.

❑ Curriculum and lesson planning.

❑ Special education laws and administrative responsibilities.

❑ Assessment procedures.

❑ School and district policies and procedures.

❑ Organization and time management techniques.

❑ Collaboration with professional colleagues, including paraeducators, and parents.

Orientation and Training: Mentor Teachers

Mentor teachers have access to professional development in the following areas:

❑ Role and expectations of the mentor.

❑ Needs of beginning special educators.

❑ Role and responsibilities of beginning special educators in the mentoring process.

❑ Effective communication skill development incorporating adult learning principles.

❑ Consultation and collaboration strategies, including solving problems, giving constructive feedback, and providing social support.

❑ Time management and organizational strategies.

❑ Classroom observation skills.

❑ Updates on IEP development and program implementation.

❑ Updates on special education laws and administrative requirements.

❑ Advising and coaching skills.

❑ Behavior management strategies across grade levels and disabilities.

❑ Instructional strategies, including accommodations and modifications for content.

☐ The Mentoring Induction Checklist (page 3 of 4)

Roles and Responsibilities of the Mentoring Team

Mentor teacher:

- ☐ Works with only one beginning special educator per year.
- ☐ Has opportunity to meet regularly with other mentors to share materials, strategies, successes, and concerns.
- ☐ Attends all professional development and orientation sessions.
- ☐ Provides support and guidance.
- ☐ Acclimates the beginning special educator to school and community culture.
- ☐ Observes the beginning teacher regularly.
- ☐ Provides post-observation feedback in a timely manner.
- ☐ Models appropriate classroom and professional behaviors.
- ☐ Models reflective practices.
- ☐ Maintains a professional and confidential relationship.
- ☐ Participates in evaluation of the program.

Beginning teacher:

- ☐ Attends all professional development and orientation sessions.
- ☐ Requests assistance proactively.
- ☐ Schedules and attends sessions with mentor teacher.
- ☐ Remains open and responsive to feedback/suggestions.
- ☐ Observes other teachers.
- ☐ Conducts self-assessment and uses reflective skills.
- ☐ Participates in evaluation of mentoring program.

☐ The Mentoring Induction Checklist (page 4 of 4)

Mentor coordinator:

❐ Manages the mentoring program.

❐ Ensures building administrators are informed and supportive.

❐ Develops district recommended procedures for mentoring.

❐ Guides development and adoption of resource materials and schedules inservice training for beginning special educators and mentors.

❐ Arranges and conducts regular meetings with new teachers and mentors.

❐ Ensures implementation, evaluation, and improvement of mentoring program.

❐ Helps provide more intensive support for individual special education and mentor teachers as needed.

Building administrator:

❐ Attends orientation session on mentoring implementation.

❐ Provides release time for beginning special educators and mentors to observe and conference with each other.

❐ Observes and facilitates mentoring relationships.

❐ Nominates only master teachers as mentors.

❐ Offers to reduce responsibilities of beginning special educators.

❐ Offers to reduce responsibilities of mentors.

❐ Is supportive of mentors and publicly recognizes the contributions of mentors.

❐ Finds ways to support new teachers and create a positive school climate.

❐ Assumes responsibility for formal evaluation of new teachers beginning within the first semester that is separate from mentoring program.

❐ Participates in evaluation of the mentoring program.

Notes:

■ Chapter Three
New Teachers

The Heart of a Mentoring Program

Learn About...

■ **Beginning Teacher Needs**

■ **Supporting Beginning Special Education Teachers**

■ **Mentoring Responsibilities of Beginning Teachers**

■ **Becoming a Reflective Teacher**

■ **Self-Assessment**

The goal and intent of mentoring programs for special educators is to provide the resources necessary for first year special education teachers to be successful. In establishing any mentoring program, this goal should be foremost; it should drive all other activities that are selected as components for the mentoring program. The beginning teacher is the heart and the focal point of the mentoring program.

■ *The Needs of Beginning Special Education Teachers*

Beginning teachers can have a variety of needs. New special education teachers face many unique challenges that range from mastering the technicalities of IEPs, to learning how to collaborate with general education teachers, to being the teacher of record. Akron Public Schools (2002) identified the following needs that typically require assistance from mentors:

- Managing the classroom.

- Acquiring systems information.

- Obtaining instructional resources.

- Planning, organizing, and managing work.

- Assessing student work.

- Motivating students.

- Using effective teaching methods.

- Addressing individual student needs and interests.

- Dealing with student problems.

- Communicating with colleagues.
- Communicating with parents.
- Adjusting to the teaching environment
- Receiving emotional support.

In comparison to general educators, new special educators face many unique challenges. These challenges must be considered in designing and operating a mentoring program.

Some difficulties arise when a mismatch occurs between the special education teacher's training, experience, and job placement. Such mismatches may include:

- Expecting to teach small groups of children and, instead, being assigned to co-teaching general education classes.
- Being prepared for elementary school and then being placed at the secondary level.
- Being prepared to work with students with learning disabilities and then being employed to work with students with emotional problems.

Special education teachers also report being overwhelmed with paperwork, feeling isolated, and lacking adequate support from administrators (Kozleski, Mainzer, & Deshler, 2001). Time management is difficult for them, particularly when caseloads are large. Mentors may want to spend time helping new teachers manage their time. The text box, *Tips for Time Management* offers discussion points and insights that can be shared with new teachers.

New special education teachers also may be faced with students who present some of the greatest academic and behavioral challenges (Griffin et al., 2003; Kozleski, Mainzer, & Deshler, 2001; White 1995). Mentors can help beginning teachers set positive expectations, explicit rules, and clear routines for the classroom. The following types of information can be shared with new teachers during initial professional development sessions to help them establish more effective classroom environments and improve their success as new teachers.

Planning

Effective teachers plan for student success. They create links between the student's world and academic subjects. They help students work toward mastery by ensuring sufficient structure, appropriate sequence of information, and adequate review of material. Lessons are designed to build toward success and higher level understanding.

Effective teachers have positive expectations of students and they communicate those expectations to students. They also pace instruction so that students stay engaged. Students arrive at school expecting that teachers will make a difference in their lives.

Mentors may want to ask new teachers the following questions:

- What positive expectations do you have for your students? How do you share those expectations with students and parents?
- How do you convey your expectations in the classroom? How do other teachers in the building convey positive expectations?

Organization

Effective teachers are organized. They consider space limitations and room conditions as they arrange furniture and schedule activities. Effective teachers post an assignment daily, in the same consistent location, before students enter the classroom.

Effective teachers use clear rules and procedures to structure the environment. Rules and procedures often reduce discipline problems. Student success is enhanced when they are taught the procedures and routines directly.

Teachers create a caring atmosphere in which students feel welcome. It is important to welcome students on the first day of school. Standing at the door is one way to do so.

❑ Tips for Time Management

In the Classroom

- There is an art and a science to balancing the amount of time spent on each skill and topic. The secret is sufficient time for understanding, but not so much time that students have time to waste or get bored.
- Different activities will merit different amounts of time. Go deep and spend more time on some topics than others.
- Time spent on discipline and misbehavior detracts from instructional time. Routines, procedures, schoolwide rules, and consistency all will reduce the amount of time taken away from instruction.
- Pick your battles. If you choose to provide consequences for each misbehavior, your time can be consumed with negativity.
- Time spent planning can result in time saved in the classroom. Effective lesson planning can result in more rapid learning and success.
- Find a few lessons that work well and analyze how you put those lessons together. Then repeat that formula. This will save planning time.
- Timing is important! Start lessons with warm-ups, build interest, and then wrap up with conclusions or next steps. Pace activities to reflect student needs, attention span, and the importance of the topic or skill being learned.

In Planning

- Realize that new, different, innovative, and creative are not always what is needed. Plan some lessons that will be oriented toward drill and practice. This not only saves you planning time, but can result in better student fluency and mastery.
- Plan with peers. Share lessons and piggyback on their success.
- Get students to help with planning and delivery of instruction.
- Look at web sites that provide lesson plans.
- Whenever possible plan at least a week in advance.
- Save time by planning for the exceptions. For example, be prepared to modify instruction for students who are struggling or who need more advanced work.
- Consider the rhythm of the week. Mondays are for getting back into the swing of things. By Friday, we're all ready for a break. Also consider the rhythm of the day and the instructional period or the season.
- Plan for routines and procedures. These will help guide your class.

In Mentoring and Induction

- Set aside time to plan with your mentor.
- Take time to reflect on your teaching.
- Find time for your mentor to observe you and for you to observe a variety of teachers.

Note: This text box was reprinted with the permission of Christine Mason, Director, Transition to Teaching project, Student Support Center, Washington, DC. ©2006

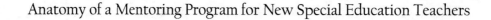

Mentors may want to ask new teachers the following questions:

- How have you organized your classroom for success?

- What typically happens when a teacher has difficulty locating materials? What can you do to prevent that from occurring?

- How do other teachers in the building use bookshelves, tables, boxes, etc. to stay organized?

- What procedures, routines, and rules have you established? How successful are they in helping students stay on task? What is an effective procedure for getting a student's attention?

- What do you do when one or more students are not following the routine or procedure you have established in your classroom?

- How do you greet students each day?

Mentors also may help beginning teachers reflect on their classroom management skills. One technique has beginning teachers keep track of the times during the day when students present problems. These data can lead to insights about the types of skills and knowledge needed by the beginning teacher.

Establishing Rules

An important part of teaching is to ensure that classroom rules and procedures are made explicit to students. The text box, *Checklist for Rules and Routines*, can be given to new special education teachers to help them plan. The items in the checklist prompt new teachers to reflect on rules and procedures that must be taught and established in well structured classrooms. This information also is useful for general education teachers working in inclusive and/or co-teaching settings.

Acclimating to the School

Teachers who are new to the profession and new to a geographic area also need support and assistance in becoming acclimated to their schools and communities. They need to understand the dynamics of their environment and how to contribute most effectively in that environment.

To meet their needs, new teachers want mentors who are trustworthy and readily available, preferably within their building. Special educators need special educators as mentors. First-year teachers also want information on district policies regarding IEPs and paperwork, as well as assistance locating supplies, obtaining classroom materials, planning instruction, working with parents and colleagues, and assessing student learning (White & Mason, 2002).

New teachers working with mentors create a critical team as the heart and soul of the program. The team is characterized by respect for the role that each player takes and a strengthening of the skills of each member of the team. The philosophy that teachers' skills fall along a continuum of development acknowledges the freshness a beginning teacher brings to the classroom, while respecting the achievements of the veteran or master teacher (Billingsley, 2002). Regardless of experience, all teachers can benefit from professional development opportunities that meet their specific needs and are presented in a manner that encourages participation.

■ *Supporting the Beginning Special Education Teacher*

Beginning special educators, like other teachers, are most successful when they are supported. Frequent collegial interaction among new and experienced teachers—including team planning, sharing, evaluation, and learning—are important components of such learning communities. These interactions contribute to greater self-confidence and stronger professional identities for new teachers (Feiman-Nemser, Carville, Schwille, & Yusko, 2000; Wanzare & da Costa 2000). Support may include, but is not limited to, shared responsibility where teachers and administrators share values and goals, a climate of professionalism prevails, and opportunities for professional development are fostered (Bartholomay, Wallace, & Mason, 2001; Billingsley, 2002; Billingsley & Tomchin, 1992; Boyer & Lee, 2001; Brownell & Smith, 1993; Carter & Scruggs, 2001; Griffin et al., 2003; Kozleski, Mainzer, & Deshler, 2001; Mastropieri, 2001).

☐ Checklist for Rules and Routines

Expectations

Students understand:

- ☐ The seating plan.

- ☐ What they are expected to bring to class (e.g., paper, pencils, class notebook, homework, assignment book, etc.).

- ☐ Where to look for assignments (e.g., write each lesson on the chalkboard, etc.).

- ☐ What is expected of them when they enter the classroom (e.g., place personal belongings in desk, locker, or bookshelf, etc.; copy classwork from chalkboard; etc.).

- ☐ Rules for visiting with friends (e.g., before the class starts).

Procedures

Students have been taught the procedures for:

- ☐ Requesting a drink of water.

- ☐ Going to the restroom.

- ☐ Going to the office.

- ☐ Going to their locker.

- ☐ Asking for assistance.

- ☐ Sharpening pencils and requesting supplies.

- ☐ What to do if they are late to class.

- ☐ What they should do if they need to remove themselves from class (e.g., emotional problem).

- ☐ How to leave the classroom (e.g., they may leave when the bell rings, they may leave only when dismissed by the teacher, etc.).

Rules Related to Materials and Textbooks

Students have been taught:

- ☐ The requirements for book covers.

- ☐ How to care for materials.

- ☐ What materials to bring to class.

- ☐ What they should do if they do not have their materials.

Policies for Classwork

Students have been taught:

- ☐ Where and when completed work should be turned in.

- ☐ How work will be discussed.

- ☐ Where to keep their work in the classroom (e.g., file folders, portfolio, etc.).

- ☐ The format for heading papers (e.g., where name and date are written).

- ☐ When talking is allowed.

- ☐ How late assignments are handled.

- ☐ How assignments are graded.

- ☐ How bonus points or extra credit are earned.

Rules for Behavior

- ☐ Students have been taught schoolwide rules.

- ☐ Classroom rules are stated positively, posted prominently, and enforced fairly.

- ☐ Students are aware of teacher signals (e.g., to quiet down, etc.).

Note: This text box was reprinted with the permission of Christine Mason, Director, Transition to Teaching project, Student Support Center, Washington, DC. ©2006

Beginning special education teachers should be considered professionals, not student teachers. New teachers develop by evaluating their own teaching styles and effectiveness, not just by mimicking what they are seeing in their mentor or in other teachers. Offering social support puts beginning teachers at ease; offering professional support advances their knowledge base; and supporting their practice makes them more confident educators (Feiman-Nemser, 1992). New teachers also need initial and ongoing training. Professional development activities must be selected specifically to match the needs of new teachers with their ability to use the information provided.

> *"I went to a two-day work session on curriculum before school started and got all these great curriculum manuals—hundreds and hundreds of pages long! I was so excited and then I went to my new classroom and saw that it was empty—no chairs, no desks, and no books. Those great curriculum guides didn't do me much good, except some of the students did use them as chairs the first few days."*
>
> **—New Teacher,
> Mentoring Induction Project**

Beginning teachers should participate in an initial mentoring inservice as soon as possible—prior to the beginning of the school year if possible. In addition to formal professional development, they should have the opportunity to meet regularly with other new teachers to share materials, strategies, successes, and concerns. The text box, *How Akron Public Schools Orients New Special Education Teachers*, provides an example.

In the Mentoring Induction Project, school districts offered a wide array of supports. Examples include:

❑ How Akron Public Schools Orients New Special Education Teachers

Akron Public Schools in Ohio offers new special education teacher seminars each year. All special education staff who have been hired within the past three years are invited to attend. The seminars are held after school and last about two hours. Topics may include:

- Classroom management.
- Effective teaching strategies.
- Working with students who have Attention Deficit/Hyperactivity Disorder.
- Establishing classroom procedures and routines.
- Communicating with parents.
- Working with education assistants.

Discussion groups on specific disability areas are led by mentor teachers.

All entry year teachers must attend four out of five new teacher meetings. Veteran teachers who are new to the district also are encouraged to attend the sessions. Mentors are invited to attend with their new teachers.

- Teacher inservice academies on topics such as IEP development, evaluation, and behavior management.

- Newsletters with "timely tips" on such topics as handling the first day of school, preparing for teacher-parent conferences, and reducing teacher stress. Mentors should share ideas and suggestions with new teachers. The text boxes, *Suggestions for Back-to-School Night* and *Ideas for Parent-Teacher Conferences*, can be shared with new teachers as they plan for these events.

- Opportunities to attend professional conferences, observe master teachers, and develop their own self-improvement plans.

New teachers in the Mentoring Induction Project reported that they wanted more training in areas related specifically to special education. Examples follow:

- Development and implementation of IEPs.

- Special education laws and paperwork.

- Assessment procedures.

- Techniques for working with parents and teaching assistants.

■ *Responsibilities of Beginning Teachers in the Mentoring Program*

The beginning special education teacher plays an active role in the mentoring relationship. Specific beginning teacher responsibilities include:

- Attending all professional development and orientation sessions relevant to mentoring.

- Requesting assistance proactively related to teaching.

- Understanding the school and community culture.

- Working with other school personnel.

- Scheduling and attending sessions with the mentor teacher to discuss progress and any concerns.

- Remaining open and responsive to feedback and suggestions from the mentor.

- Observing other experienced teachers, including the mentor teacher.

- Conducting self-assessments and using reflective skills to enhance teaching and classroom management skills.

- Participating in the evaluation of the mentoring program.

Some school districts—such as the Clark County School System in Nevada—provide booklets detailing new teacher responsibilities, along with suggestions and resources. For example, the Clark County School System organizes suggestions around the following topics:

- Prior to the first day of school (e.g., making contacts, setting up folders, reviewing IEPs, preparing lessons, reviewing school documents, organizing the classroom, familiarizing oneself with assistants, etc.).

- First days and weeks of school (e.g., reviewing IEPs with general educators, learning about students, establishing classroom management system, collaborating with other teachers, etc.).

Mentors, as well as administrators, should locate district documents and share them with new teachers. If the school district does not have such documents, consider developing them or purchasing them from a commercial publisher. The Council for Exceptional Children has published an excellent resource that also can be used for this purpose. The reference is:

> Burnette, J., & Peters-Johnson, C. (Eds.). *Thriving as a special educator: Balancing your practices and ideals.* Arlington, VA: Council for Exceptional Children. Learn more about the book online at **www.cec.sped.org**.

In addition, mentors and administrators should provide practical resources on topics such as differentiating instruction, managing behavior, establishing classroom rules, co-teaching, making accommodations, communicating with families, and writing IEPs. Such resources should become the focus of professional development sessions. New teachers also should be encouraged to share resources with general education teachers with whom they are co-teaching and/or collaborating.

❑ Suggestions for Back-to-School Night

Involve the students in preparing for the event. Suggestions include:

- Have students put together a portfolio of work they have selected.

- Have students work together on a mural, a report, or a multi-media presentation. Showcase these.

- Have students prepare invitations. If students are involved in preparing for the event and enthusiastic about inviting their parents, parents are more likely to attend.

- Have students help decorate the room. Post artwork and exemplary papers.

Deliver good news. Suggestions include:

- Let parents know the positives about their child and the class.

- Tell parents your expectations for what their child will accomplish this year.

Address parent needs. Suggestions include:

- Find ways to help parents with babysitting and transportation.

- Consider what parents will need to know to contribute to a successful school year. This might include information on homework; helping their child study; and establishing a time, place, and routine for completing homework. For younger children, this might also include reading together.

Invite parents to become resources. Suggestions include:

- Consider ways to make your school a welcoming environment for parents. For example, is there a designated room at the school where parents can meet, socialize with other parents, and engage in school-related activities?

- Invite parents to help with tutoring, school parties, and field trips.

- Consider conducting a parent survey to find out what parents would like to do.

- Listen to parents and help them feel welcome. Learn from them and be sensitive to their situations.

Describe your expectations and your plans for the year. Suggestions include:

- Curriculum that will be covered.

- Classroom and school rules.

- Grading policies.

- When you will be contacting parents and when you would like them to contact you. Convey the idea of being a team and working together for their child.

- How parents can help their child do well in school, including being positive about school, showing interest, and watching bedtime so that students are in bed early enough to get a good rest.

☐ Ideas for Parent-Teacher Conferences (page 1 of 2)

Prior to the conference, plan to:

- Meet at a conference table, not at your desk. Your desk may be perceived as a symbol of power.

- Place the table in a private part of the room away from the door.

- Use adult-sized furniture. Sit at the same level as the parent.

- Set up a comfortable waiting area for those parents who arrive early. It should be out of the weather and out of earshot of the conference in progress. For example, keep several large chairs outside the classroom. You may even want to have a table with coffee, tea, water, or juice with a "Help Yourself While You Wait" sign.

- Post a notice on the door so you are not interrupted.

- Have paper and pencils available for parents who choose to keep notes.

- Have a box of tissues within easy reach.

- Prepare questions and topics you wish to discuss.

- List academic strengths and areas that need improvement.

- Collect samples of student work and place them in a folder/portfolio.

- Have your grade and plan books available.

- Have sample textbooks and materials available for parents to see.

- Arrange student folders according to your conference schedule.

- Be sure there is student work on display in the classroom.

- Inspect your room—it should be neat and tidy. Have students clean their desks.

- Have puzzles, toys, crayons, etc. ready in case the parent brings a younger sibling.

- Dress for success.

During the conference, plan to:

- Greet the parent by name with a firm handshake at the door. Make the parent feel comfortable.

- Use language that is respectful to the parent, the child, and their culture.

- Avoid using educational jargon.

- Be as objective as possible, but show a feeling of empathy and a sense of concern. Attempt to place yourself in the parent's shoes.

- Accept the parent's view of the child and then cautiously reconstruct it to a incorporate your own picture. Keep in mind that a teacher's view is only one perspective.

- Begin with positive information and student strengths.

- Avoid comparing the child with other children or siblings.

- Be very careful in making broad generalizations about a child (i.e., "All boys are like that"). Do not make it easy to be misquoted.

☐ Ideas for Parent-Teacher Conferences (page 2 of 2)

- Don't do all the talking—be an active listener, too. Listen 60 percent and talk 40 percent. Remember, you are trying to build a collaborative relationship. Keep on the subject. Always bring the conversation back to the student.

- Paraphrase statements so you correctly interpret what the parent is saying.

- Give the parent ample opportunity to ask questions and share concerns.

- If you have no suggestions for improving a bad trait, do not bring it up.

- Don't send the parent away loaded down with countless suggestions. Concentrate on one or two things on which you can work together to help the child.

- If a parent disagrees with you or challenges you, let the parent have his or her say. At the end say, "I understand what you are saying. Let's see if we can work this out together."

- In case of unusual or strong criticism of the school by the parent, offer to arrange a conference with the principal.

- Do not simply label a student "lazy or unmotivated." Give an illustration, "Janie sat for 20 minutes yesterday looking out of the window and did not do her spelling assignment." Let the parent draw conclusions.

- Be professional. It is unethical to criticize another teacher in discussions with a parent.

- Assist the parent in searching for answers that you are not able to give. "I don't know, but I'll help you find out" is better than avoiding the question.

- Above all, relax and enjoy getting acquainted.

- Summarize any decisions made at the close of the conference.

- Encourage continued communication. Say, "Please call any time you have a concern."

- End the conference on a positive note. Say, "Thank you for coming and sharing."

After the conference, plan to:

- Make a few notes to remind yourself of important points discussed.

- Write a thank you note to the parent for attending and sharing information.

- If you need to follow up on any questions or concerns, it's best to do so as soon as possible after the conference so you do not forget.

- You might find it helpful to send out questionnaire to parents after the conference to get their feedback (e.g., what they liked, disliked, had concerns about, etc.). Be sure to mention the confidentiality of their answers and stress how much you want to work as a team.

- Don't discuss your parent conferences in front of the staff—remember confidentiality!

■ *Reflective Teaching Practices*

Mentoring will be most successful when beginning teachers take initiative in bringing concerns to mentors for problem solving and when these teachers take time to reflect on their teaching. Many mentoring programs include a component for journaling and self-assessment.

With the Mentoring Induction Project, new teachers kept a log of their meetings with mentors, including a running list of topics covered. They also conducted periodic self-assessments. From these self-assessments, new teachers can establish their own goals for improvement. Reflection logs also can become a part of their annual professional growth plan that is typically completed each spring.

When using a reflective teaching model, teacher confidence can best be supported by taking a positive approach and asking teachers to always begin with what went well. Even if a teacher does not succeed with a particular lesson, there are usually certain components that are successful. These may include:

- How the teacher introduced the lesson.

- How a specific student question was addressed.

- How the teacher was able to establish classroom control.

New teachers should reflect on the effectiveness of their lessons. Examples of reflection questions used by the Student Support Center (**www.studentsupportcenter.org**) follow.

- Am I spending sufficient time planning?

- Are the students engaged, interested, and learning?

- Is my timing and pacing effective?

- Is there adequate depth to the instruction?

- Are my instructions clear?

- Am I organized? Do I have materials ready?

- Is class time used wisely?

- Am I fair, consistent, and caring?

- Am I providing fair, frequent, and supportive feedback?

- Is my teaching improving?

- Am I teaching to the expected standards of learning?

- Are students making adequate progress?

Beginning Special Education Teacher Self-Assessment

Working with his or her mentor, the beginning teacher can identify focus areas by making a self-assessment. These should be the new teacher's topics of greatest interest or need.

The *Mentoring Induction Project Self-Assessment Survey* is provided at the end of this chapter. A summary form also is included. The topics identified in the self-assessment will provide the basis of an action plan that will be developed jointly by the new teacher and mentor. A teacher's plan of action form also is provided.

Some mentor teachers prefer to have teachers complete self-assessments at the beginning of the year, at mid-year, and again at the end of the year. This provides an opportunity for new teachers to chart their growth over time.

☐ Mentoring Induction Project Self-Assessment Form (page 1 of 3)

Mentoring Induction Project

Self Assessment Survey

Date: _____

Code: _____

MIP USE ONLY

This instrument is designed to measure how you feel about your professional skills at this particular time in your career. The information you provide on this form will not be used for any evaluation or assessment purposes. Your responses will be confidential and coded anonymously.

There are two parts to this survey. In the middle of the chart is a skill statement.

On the left side is a scale for "skill importance" and on the right side a scale for "confidence level." On the left side, please indicate how important you feel this skill is for a beginning special education teacher using the scale of 1 to 5 with:

1= This skill is **not at all important** to a beginning special education teacher.
2= This skill is **not very important** to a beginning special education teacher.
3= This skill is **somewhat important** to a beginning special education teacher.
4= This skill is **very important** to a beginning special education teacher.
5= This skill is **extremely important** to a beginning special education teacher.

On the right side, please indicate how confident you are that you have and can use this skill at this particular time in your career using the scale of 1 to 5 with:

1= I am **not at all confident** that I have and can use this skill at this time.
2= I am **not very confident** that I have and can use this skill at this time.
3= I am **somewhat confident** that I have and can use this skill at this time.
4= I am **very confident** that I have and can use this skill at this time.
5= I am **extremely confident** that I have and can use this skill at this time.

SKILL STATEMENT

1 Not at all important	2 Not very important	3 Somewhat important	4 Very important	5 Extremely important	SKILL STATEMENT	1 Not at all confident	2 Not very confident	3 Somewhat confident	4 Very confident	5 Extremely confident
1	2	3	4	5	1. Conducting instructional and other professional activities consistent with the requirements of law, rules and regulations, and local district policies and procedures.	1	2	3	4	5
1	2	3	4	5	2. Creating and maintaining records (pertaining to assessment, diagnosis, and evaluation).	1	2	3	4	5
1	2	3	4	5	3. Using various types of assessment procedures appropriately.	1	2	3	4	5

☐ Mentoring Induction Project Self-Assessment Form (page 2 of 3)

1 Not at all confident	2 Not very confident	3 Somewhat confident	4 Very confident	5 Extremely confident		1 Not at all important	2 Not very important	3 Somewhat important	4 Very important	5 Extremely important
1	2	3	4	5	4. Interpreting information from formal and informal assessment instruments and procedures.	1	2	3	4	5
1	2	3	4	5	5. Reporting assessment results to individuals with exceptional learning needs, parents, administrators, and other professionals using appropriate communication skills.	1	2	3	4	5
1	2	3	4	5	6. Developing individualized assessment strategies for instruction.	1	2	3	4	5
1	2				7. Using assessment information in making instructional decisions and planning individual programs that result in appropriate placement and intervention for all individuals with exceptional learning needs, including those from culturally and/or linguistically diverse backgrounds.	1	2	3	4	5
1	2	3	4	5	8. Evaluating the results of instruction.	1	2	3	4	5
1	2	3	4	5	9. Interpreting and using assessment data for instruction.	1	2	3	4	5
1	2	3	4	5	10. Developing and/or selecting instructional content, materials, resources, and strategies that respond to cultural, linguistic, and gender differences.	1	2	3	4	5
1	2	3	4	5	11. Preparing appropriate lesson plans.	1	2	3	4	5
1	2	3	4	5	12. Selecting, adapting, and using instructional strategies and materials according to characteristics of the learner.	1	2	3	4	5
1	2	3	4	5	13. Using instructional time properly.	1	2	3	4	5
1	2	3	4	5	14. Creating a safe, positive, and supportive learning environment in which diversities are valued.	1	2	3	4	5
1	2	3	4	5	15. Preparing and organizing materials to implement daily lesson plans.	1	2	3	4	5

☐ Mentoring Induction Project Self-Assessment Form (page 3 of 3)

1 Not at all important	2 Not very important	3 Somewhat important	4 Very important	5 Extremely important	Item	1 Not at all confident	2 Not very confident	3 Somewhat confident	4 Very confident	5 Extremely confident
1	2	3	4	5	16. Designing a learning environment that encourages active participation by learners in a variety of individual and group learning activities.	1	2	3	4	5
1	2	3	4	5	17. Designing, structuring, and managing daily routines effectively, including transition time for students, other staff, and the instructional setting.	1	2	3	4	5
1	2	3	4	5	18. Directing, observing, evaluating, and providing feedback to paraeducator.	1	2	3	4	5
1	2	3	4	5	19. Demonstrating a variety of effective behavior management techniques appropriate to the needs of individuals with exceptional learning needs.	1	2	3	4	5
1	2	3	4	5	20. Modifying the learning environment (schedule and physical arrangement) to manage inappropriate behaviors.	1	2	3	4	5
1	2	3	4	5	21. Integrating social skills into the curriculum.	1	2	3	4	5
1	2	3	4	5	22. Using collaborative strategies in working with individuals with exceptional learning needs, parents, and school and community personnel in various learning environments.	1	2	3	4	5
1	2	3	4	5	23. Planning and conducting collaborative conferences with individuals with exceptional learning needs and families or primary caregivers.	1	2	3	4	5
1	2	3	4	5	24. Collaborate with regular classroom teachers and other school and community personnel in integrating individuals with exceptional learning needs into various learning environments.	1	2	3	4	5
1	2	3	4	5	25. Communicating with regular teachers, administrators, and other school personnel about characteristics and needs of individuals with specific exceptional learning needs.	1	2	3	4	5
1	2	3	4	5	26. Practicing within the CEC Code of Ethics and other standards and policies of the profession.	1	2	3	4	5

☐ Self-Assessment Summary

Reflect on your self-assessment. For each activity, identify your strengths and/or areas for growth.

Activity	Strengths	Areas for Growth
Creating and maintaining an effective environment for all students.		
Planning instruction and designing learning experiences for all students.		
Engaging and supporting all students in learning.		
Assessing student learning.		
Understanding and organizing subject matter knowledge for student learning.		
Developing as a professional special educator.		

☐ **Action Plan**

Reflect on your self-assessment summary. For each area of growth, develop a goal. Identify steps you will take to achieve each goal.

Goal	Steps to Achieving Goal
	1. 2. 3. 4. 5.
	1. 2. 3. 4. 5.
	1. 2. 3. 4. 5.
	1. 2. 3. 4. 5.

■ Chapter Four

Effective Mentor Teachers

The Central Nervous System of a Mentoring Program

Learn About...

■ **Successful Mentors**

■ **Mentor Training**

■ **Mentor Teacher Roles and Responsibilities**

■ **Effective Mentoring**

■ **Adult Learning Principles**

■ **Positive Expectations**

■ **Coping with Stress**

■ **Observations and Conferencing**

■ **Reflecting**

Mentors, like the central nervous system, carry messages to teachers that relay optimism, confidence, and support. To do this, mentors must be alert to the climate in the new teacher's classroom, the rapport he or she is building with students, and how well he or she is adapting to the school culture. Mentors also should be sensitive to how the new teacher perceives reality.

Mentors have the opportunity to have a positive and enduring influence on the experiences and success of new special education teachers. Effective mentors indicate that assisting new teachers is a rewarding professional experience, that it feels good to give back to their profession, and that mentoring renews their enthusiasm for teaching. Mentors can improve new teacher morale, which ultimately can enhance educational experiences for students.

Mentors also report that the job is not easy. They face innumerable challenges related to finding the time to observe and conference; they are sometimes faced with how to help a teacher critique a less-than-adequate lesson; and sometimes they even find it hard to figure out where to begin when the needs of the new teacher are too great.

Mentor teachers should be master teachers—teachers with wisdom, experience, knowledge, and competence in their particular area of teaching They also should have a minimum of three to five years of teaching experience in their district. However, being a master teacher is not a guarantee that an individual will be a successful mentor. It takes a strong and wise professional to be an effective mentor.

Mentoring a colleague is very different from teaching children. Teachers, when working with students, often evaluate a student's work and then direct the student to the next task. The mentor's job does not involve evaluation of the new teacher. In fact, evaluation can hamper the relationship. Mentors accomplish much through coaching and guiding teachers through a process of self-reflection.

In the best circumstances, new special educators and mentors should be as carefully matched as the heart and central nervous system, but that may not always be possible. If the new teacher's classroom has a student population that is very different from the mentor's, the mentor may have to support the new teacher through challenges that he or she has not experienced. Or, the beginning teacher may have been trained to work with curricula in a way that is unfamiliar to the mentor.

Mentors need to be able to share their concerns and get advice from other mentors. They should be able to rely on inservice training that prepares them for circumstances such as these.

The mentor teacher plays the most crucial role in mentoring programs (Feiman-Nemser, 1992; Little, 1990; Whitaker, 2000; White, 1995). To achieve desired outcomes with mentoring, great care must be taken in establishing the criteria for mentors and in matching mentors with new teachers (Little, 1990; White, 1995).

Mentors can be drawn from a variety of environments in the school district. They typically are nominated by the principal, who also recommends the mentor/teacher match. The characteristics of this match are important—if the heart and central nervous system of mentoring are to function as a team, their personalities must mesh and they must understand each other.

■ *Successful Mentor Teachers*

What makes a successful mentor teacher? Successful mentors must be:

- Sensitive to the needs of the new teacher.

- Able to assess what will be most valuable for the new teacher's development.

- Astute observers and communicators.

- Aware of nonverbal communication cues from the new teacher.

- Able to provide guidance in a tactful way.

> *"They'll no longer come to you with issues or problems if they feel that their job could be on the line. They've got to feel safe, non-threatened, and secure. They may have some questions that they think may be silly or ridiculous. If they have to evaluate whether they can ask those questions or share things, then you're not a mentor."*
>
> **—Mentor Teacher, Mentoring Induction Project**

Like the central nervous system, the mentor is an integrating factor. The mentor uses input from the environment to strengthen the new teacher's skills.

Successful mentors possess strong character—they are trustworthy, approachable, supportive, positive, good listeners, patient, sensitive, confident, and professional (Whitaker, 2000; White & Mason, 2002). They possess professional characteristics that include advocating for students with disabilities, knowing what is expected of new teachers, knowing their role as mentors, and modeling professional responsibility and behavior.

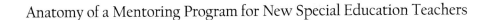

When it comes to experience, the most successful mentors for special education teachers are special educators themselves, preferably teaching at the same school with the same type of students at the same age or grade level (White & Mason, 2006). If that is not possible, then these qualities should be prioritized in the order listed, beginning with the requirement that the mentor must be a special educator.

In the Mentoring Induction Project pilot sites, 71 percent of the new teachers and mentors were in the same school, 81 percent taught the same type of students, and 60 percent taught at the same age or grade level. Finally, the most successful mentors were master teachers with three to five years of experience in their current school districts, had been trained to mentor, and had volunteered for the assignment (Council for Exceptional Children, 1997; Huling-Austin, 1992; Whitaker, 2000; White, 1995; White & Mason, 2002).

For mentor teachers, mentoring is a professional development activity that can be a catalyst to their own growth and the refinement of their classroom skills. It helps them refine their knowledge and learn about communicating with others who do not possess their skills. Their commitment to teaching is renewed. In their own self-reflection, they can recall their first days and weeks of teaching, remembering what drew them into the field. They can remember the things they wish someone had told them that would have eased their transition. When mentors in a district come together for sharing and support, they have opportunities to solve problems, to learn how to coach a teacher who may be resistant to accepting the advice, and to discuss how to help a teacher who is experiencing difficulties.

In some mentoring programs, some of the most talented teachers in the school district are mentors. Often, these teachers are individuals who have won awards for their teaching. They may be interested in pursing advanced education, perhaps even becoming curriculum specialists, consultant teachers, principals, or directors of special education. The power of the effectiveness of a talented mentor, particularly one who is guided through a systematic mentoring program with adequate feedback and direction, cannot be over-

stated. Mentors make a difference in improving the morale of new teachers, as well as increasing academic achievement and enhancing educational experiences for students.

■ *Mentor Training*

Mentors need an orientation to mentoring as well as updates to ensure that they are ready to provide new teachers with the most current information and approaches. Often, districts will arrange for mentors to receive professional development or university credit for the mentoring courses they take. Orientation should begin prior to the first meeting with new teachers, and professional development inservice should be available throughout the school year.

Mentoring Induction Project mentors reported that they wanted more training in general coaching skills as well as skills specifically related to educational development. Examples included:

- Effective communication skill development incorporating adult learning principles.

- Consultation strategies, including how to give constructive feedback and provide social support.

- Time management and organizational strategies.

- Advising and coaching skills.

- Collaboration and problem-solving skills.

They also identified skills specific to the special education context. Examples included:

- The role and expectations of the mentor.

- The needs of new special education teachers and their roles and responsibilities in the mentoring process.

- Classroom observation skills.

- IEP development and implementation, changes in special education laws, and paperwork requirements.

- Behavior management strategies across grade levels and disabilities.

- Curriculum and instructional strategies.

In addition, mentor teachers wanted the opportunity to meet regularly with other mentors to share materials, strategies, successes, and concerns.

■ *Mentor Teacher Roles and Responsibilities*

Effective mentoring begins with a clear understanding of the different roles involved in providing peer support. This understanding helps the mentor develop a spirit of professionalism and friendship that builds a foundation for trust, even during the initial meetings. According to Denmark and Podsen (2000), effective mentors, in conveying their support, also will convey a sense of competence, a commitment to mentoring, and a willingness to share classroom strategies.

A mentor may be called upon to help support the new special education teacher in many and varied ways. This support can range from simply assisting with mundane tasks such as ordering classroom supplies, to understanding the intricacies of district paperwork, to helping the new teacher reflect on improving communication with parents or colleagues. Sometimes the most important thing a mentor can do is to simply listen to the new teacher. Providing emotional support to a teacher who may feel isolated is one of the most valuable contributions a mentor can make (Whitaker, 2000; White & Mason, 2002).

The mentor teacher guides, assists, and supports the beginning special education teacher during the crucial first year of teaching. Ideally, each mentor teacher should work with only one beginning special education teacher per year.

Specific responsibilities of the mentor teacher include:

- Attending all training sessions relevant to mentoring.
- Providing support and guidance to the beginning teacher in special education laws and procedures (e.g., developing IEPs, obtaining classroom materials, referral and placement procedures, behavior management, planning

and instruction, assessment, and working with parents and colleagues).

- Acclimating the beginning teacher to the culture of the school and the community.
- Observing the beginning teacher regularly.
- Providing post-observation feedback in a timely manner, preferably the same day as the observation.
- Modeling appropriate instructional techniques, classroom management, and professional behavior.
- Maintaining a professional and confidential relationship based on respect and trust.
- Participating in the evaluation of the mentoring program.

A list of questions to help mentors reflect on their upcoming responsibilities is found in the text box, *Reflection Questions: On Becoming a Mentor.*

In the Mentoring Induction Project, feedback from mentors at seven national sites showed that mentors provided both instructional and emotional support to new teachers. These mentors were particularly sensitive to some of the issues that were primary concerns of these teachers. Mentors shared general knowledge about expectations within the school district and building, and they also were available to answer more specific questions such as how to develop IEPs, how to support and discipline students with challenging behaviors, and how to modify instruction to assist students who were having difficulty understanding concepts.

■ *Effective Mentoring*

Whether providing guidance on instruction, paperwork, the school environment, or a specific student, the mentor teacher must be mindful of the characteristics that differentiate an effective from an ineffective mentor.

Based on observations of successful and unsuccessful mentoring experiences, Rowley (1999) identified the following traits of effective mentors:

☐ Reflection Questions—On Becoming a Mentor

- If you find out whom you will be mentoring prior to school beginning, what kinds of things might you do to demonstrate your support?

- The first week or two of school are usually high-stress times for entry level teachers. What are some strategies that you can use to demonstrate your support?

- During the first month, what are some things that you can do to provide ongoing support for the entry level teacher?

- As the year progresses, what kinds of support and assistance does an entry level teacher need?

- What do you do to ensure this relationship is a good one from the onset?

- What do you do if the relationship is "rocky," or the entry level teacher simply does not want to spend any time with you?

- What are some things not to do as the mentor?

- If the entry level teacher encounters difficulty, what do you do as the mentor?

- Should you involve the building principal and, if so, in what way?

From: Akron Public Schools (2002).

- **Good mentors are committed to mentoring.** They understand the needs of beginning teachers and have formal mentor training. Good mentoring can be a challenging endeavor, and good mentors recognize that it requires their persistence and dedication to the job.

- **Good mentors model continuous learning.** Rather than offer beginning teachers the right answers, mentors model their own search for better and more effective practices. Mentors also seek out high-quality professional growth experiences for themselves.

- **Good mentors accept beginning teachers.** A beginning special education teacher is a developing professional. The mentor recognizes this and is not judgmental or rejecting of him or her. The beginning teacher is accepted and nurtured throughout the program.

- **Good mentors communicate hope and optimism.** Veteran teachers who have maintained their positive outlook make the best mentors. They exhibit a genuine caring that earns the new teacher's trust, particularly during times of stress, such as early in the school year. A mentor shares his or her own struggles and capitalizes on the teacher's potential.

Portner (1999), in his text on mentoring, describes the four primary functions of the mentor. They are:

- **Relating.** An effective mentor makes him or herself available to new teachers, makes practical suggestions, and works on building trust and respect while maintaining a sense of professionalism. To establish a sense of trust, the mentor must respect the need for confidentiality, express his or her own feelings as well as thoughts, and use descriptive rather than evaluative or judgmental statements. The mentor also should be mindful of nonverbal communication and the body language of the new teacher. While the new teacher may not verbalize discomfort, discomfort with certain observations, recommendations, or feedback may be demonstrated by the tone or vagueness of responses, failure to follow through on planned meetings, or body language. The mentor must use care to avoid overloading the new teacher with feedback that is too detailed or attempts to cover too much ground. The mentor must listen respectfully. Sometimes being a sounding board for the new teacher is more important than providing detailed instructions or specific guidance.

- **Assessing.** It is important to begin the year by working with the new teacher to complete a self-assessment survey or questionnaire with the new teacher and develop a joint plan of action. The mentor then uses the information from that survey to pinpoint areas the new teacher would like to strengthen, providing a foundation for the observations and conferencing that follow. While the number of observations will vary with the new teacher's needs, the mentor should observe the beginning teacher several times during the course of the year, with an observation conference scheduled as soon as possible after each observation.

- **Coaching.** In order to be an effective coach, mentors may wish to model or demonstrate how to teach a particular lesson or how to handle a certain behavior. Rather than presenting information in terms of absolutes, it helps to provide alternatives or to ask the new teacher to provide them, helping him or her weigh the benefits and implement the recommendations.

- **Guiding.** Effective mentors, during the course of the year, assist new teachers in becoming self-reflective and assuming responsibility for conducting self-critiques and building new skills. In this way, rather than making decisions for the teacher, the mentor guides the new teacher through a process of self-reflection.

■ *Using Adult Learning Principles in Mentoring*

Mentors can be more effective if they apply principles of adult learning as they work with new teachers. For example, they should:

- Choose a conference location that is quiet, private, and free of distractions.

- Avoid covering too much too quickly.

- Spend enough time listening to the new teacher.

- Start and end with positive comments.

- Provide positive feedback.

- Be quick to acknowledge improvements.

Adult learners are self-motivated—new teachers will benefit from opportunities to critique their own lessons rather than having the mentor be too critical or too directive. A self-discovery approach is often best. New teachers need a chance to discover for themselves what works for them. The mentor can provide tools for the teacher to practice new strategies and reflect on his or her performance. Instead of presenting only one way to do something, suggest alternatives. In some instances, the mentor also may want to recommend consulting someone who might be a better resource for specific issues or concerns, and to share other resources that will assist the new teacher.

"Mentoring makes me feel very lucky, very happy, and very satisfied. The little problems that come up seem so much less monumental. I realize that this is good."

—Mentor Teacher, Mentoring Induction Project

However, there are times when the mentor will want to be more directive. For example, when the mentor and new teacher are working together to achieve specific goals and the mentor provides more detailed guidance about how to achieve them. When preparing students for exams associated with the school's annual yearly progress under NCLB, a more directive approach may be especially useful.

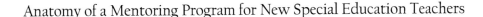

Mentors need to make sure that communication is two-way and responsive to the new teacher's concerns. They need to take time to listen. Whenever possible, they should focus discussions on the goals and topic areas identified by the new teacher. With regard to students' needs, mentors need to ask questions rather than assuming or making inferences about the students' needs or the reason the teacher organized a particular activity.

Sometimes mentors find that they are unable to schedule adequate time for observation and coaching. Should this occur, mentors can still set expectations for new teacher self-reflection and help guide the new teacher. Mentors may do this by modeling self-reflection and/or sharing their own reflections. [For more ideas on guiding self-reflections, visit the Student Support Center at **www.studentsupportcenter.org**.]

Above all, mentors need to understand that mentoring is a personal relationship. They can provide reassurance, use humor, and relate stories about other first-year teachers (including themselves) to put the teacher at ease. One self-reflection exercise for mentors is to remember their own first days and weeks of teaching and identify things they wish others had told them. These can sometimes be most useful to the new teacher. Above all, mentors must be sure to maintain confidentiality.

■ *Helping New Teachers Develop Positive Expectations*

Mentoring will be more satisfactory if both partners understand their roles and take the initiative to build an effective relationship. If the two partners share joint goals in a new teacher action plan, for example, it may be easier to handle the difficulties that arise as they attempt to meet the expectations of the mentoring program. New teachers can assist both the mentor and themselves by making time to meet with and observe the mentor teacher and other teachers in their classrooms and by proactively seeking feedback and being responsive to suggestions. New teachers who establish a pattern of self-assessment and reflection will gain experience that

will be invaluable as they find themselves in new and difficult situations throughout their teaching career.

New teachers develop positive expectations of the mentoring experience based on their involvement in the process. Examples of involving new teachers includes the following:

- Allowing them to be active participants in the mentoring process. Let the new teacher help you make arrangements for observations and conferencing. Encourage active listening, reflecting on what is being suggested, and asking questions.

- Having them complete self-assessments at the beginning of the year and work with you to develop action plans to focus on their areas of greatest interest or need.

- Having them schedule follow-up conference after observations.

- Encouraging them to take advantage of opportunities to observe other teachers.

- Encouraging them to contact you whenever they need additional help.

■ *Helping New Teachers Cope with Stress*

A mentor may need to help the new special educator cope with the stress involved in teaching—stress that can be particularly high during that first year as he or she experiments with various teaching strategies, adjusts to the needs of the students, addresses parental concerns, and tries to fit into the school culture. Some special educators, because of the nature of the students they serve, may find themselves in unusually stressful situations as they handle students with extreme behavior problems and/or challenging cognitive needs. The strength and support of their mentor can foster resilience.

In many cases, basic stress management information may be helpful. New teachers may appreciate guidance related to exercise, sleep, diet, relaxation, and sources of additional support, including family, friends, and other new teachers. (The inservice training sessions for new teachers should provide one avenue for teachers to meet and discuss common concerns.)

■ *Observations and Conferencing*

The new teacher's self-assessment can provide some direction regarding specific areas he or she would like to strengthen. Results can help guide observations by identifying specific areas of focus.

Observations can be structured in various ways. The exact nature of the observation may vary according to the requirements of the specific school district. Most districts will have observation/feedback forms. Depending upon the nature of the students' disabilities, the type of classroom (general education/resource room), and the teacher's role (lead teacher or consulting teacher), the mentor may have to make additional notes. Mentors will want to use any forms the district makes available for new teacher self-assessment to help guide the planning and feedback process.

The Akron Public Schools (2002) developed a general timeline for mentors. In the first month, mentors are asked to:

- Meet with the new teacher at least twice a week (if not practical, email or call home).

- Review the teacher's first IEP and sit in on the first meeting to provide assistance if needed.

- Arrange for the teacher to observe them teaching a lesson and to discuss the observation.

- In meetings, discuss topics such as lesson plans, materials for discussion, behavior management plans, communicating with general education teachers, working with related service providers, grouping students and instructional procedures, and making long-range plans for the year.

Throughout the first semester, the Akron School District asks mentors to:

- Meet at least weekly to discuss documentation and record keeping, grading and report cards, specific student concerns, etc.

- Arrange for the new teacher to observe other teachers at least twice.

- Meet after the observations to discuss what was learned.

- Observe the teacher at least once and provide feedback.

- Continue to provide encouragement and support.

Throughout the second semester Akron Public School mentors are expected to:

- Meet at least every other week and discuss any concerns.

- Develop end-of-year procedures and plans for next year.

- Answer any questions or refer the new teacher to someone who can.

"Benefits will vary from district to district. Participants will have a wide range of opportunities to expand their professional development as well as participate in a state network of resource personnel. Other opportunities include sharing the enjoyment of teaching; justifying one's own career decision; demonstrating a capacity to support, nurture, and influence education; and transmitting one's own values and skills."

**—Staff Developer,
Utah Personnel Development Center**

- Help the new teacher analyze student learning and instructional strategies.

- Observe the teacher at least once and provide feedback.

- Encourage the new teacher to continue to observe other teachers.

- Continue to provide encouragement and support.

As mentors work with new teachers, they will find that their effectiveness increases when they help them focus on improving only one or two areas or skills at a time. To assist teachers, in addition to observation and conferences, the mentor may want to demonstrate a particular teaching technique or strategy. Mentors also may help the teacher by asking questions of students and using their input to help guide revisions the new teacher will make. New teachers also may ask for guidance from others in the building, such as lead teachers or department chairs.

Sometimes the most effective mentoring comes about through the mentor's role as a conduit of information. Giving teachers tips about web sites, resources available within the library, or how other teachers in a building handle particular behavior problems can help the teacher not only gain new skills, but acclimate to the expectations and the culture of the school.

Mentors must always consider the unique needs of special educators. This is especially true if a mentor does not have a background in special education.

■ *Reflecting on the Role of Mentor*

Just as new teachers are asked to reflect on their new roles and responsibilities, mentor teachers may wish to reflect on their role as well. Some school districts have formal mentor assessments that offer a perfect opportunity for introspection and reflection.

Mentors may want to consider forming a collegial group with other mentors where they can share reflections on being a mentor. Conferences with administrators and mentor coordinators also can allow for sharing insights that can be used for program improvement.

The Mentoring Induction Project used the form at the end of this chapter to help mentors reflect on their roles and responsibilities.

☐ Mentor's Self-Assessment (page 1 of 4)

Mentor Teacher's Evaluation of Assistance Provided

As a mentor teacher, you have the unique experience and information needed to help determine what characteristics make mentors most effective, techniques of effective mentoring for first-year special education teachers, and the effect that mentoring may have on the professional growth of mentor teachers. Your thoughtful and honest responses to the following sets of questions will be appreciated. Your responses will be confidential and coded only by your MIP code number.

During this year, did you give the new teacher you mentored assistance with:	Circle: Y=Yes N = No If no, skip to next question.	If "YES" how much do you feel you were able to help? Circle: 1= No Help At All 2= Very Little Help 3= Moderately Helpful 4= Very Helpful 5= Extremely Helpful	If you felt there was only moderate to no help (1,2,3) do you feel it was because: Circle: 1 = there wasn't enough time 2 = new teacher wasn't responsive to help 3 = other factors
1. Paperwork associated with special education laws and procedures?	Y N	1 2 3 4 5	1 2 3
2. Developing, writing, or monitoring IEPs according to your local district regulations?	Y N	1 2 3 4 5	1 2 3
3. Obtaining classroom materials and supplies from the school or district?	Y N	1 2 3 4 5	1 2 3
4. Interpreting and using information from formal and informal assessment instruments for instructional purposes?	Y N	1 2 3 4 5	1 2 3
5. Preparing appropriate and effective lesson plans?	Y N	1 2 3 4 5	1 2 3
6. Selecting, adapting, or using instructional strategies or materials to meet the individual learning needs of the students?	Y N	1 2 3 4 5	1 2 3
7. Implementing behavior management techniques appropriate to the students' needs?	Y N	1 2 3 4 5	1 2 3
8. Procedures concerning the referral, placement, and/or reevaluation of students in that school?	Y N	1 2 3 4 5	1 2 3
9. Getting acclimated to that new school (getting to know new faculty, where things were in the building, new ways of doing things)?	Y N	1 2 3 4 5	1 2 3
10. Planning or conducting collaborative conferences with students and their families?	Y N	1 2 3 4 5	1 2 3
11. Directing and supervising the work of a paraeducator, volunteer, or tutor?	Y N	1 2 3 4 5	1 2 3
12. Personal issues (new job/career, job satisfaction, feelings of frustration, contract issues, social life, etc.)?	Y N	1 2 3 4 5	1 2 3
13. Time management (balancing professional life with personal life)?	Y N	1 2 3 4 5	1 2 3
14. Collaborating with regular classroom teachers and other school personnel about the characteristics and needs of the students, including integrating them into various learning environments?	Y N	1 2 3 4 5	1 2 3
15. Learning and utilizing the general education curriculum of your state/district?	Y N	1 2 3 4 5	1 2 3

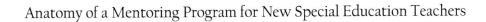

☐ Mentor's Self-Assessment (page 2 of 4)

Mentor Teacher Activity Evaluation. On the left side of the chart is an activity that could be associated with mentoring. On the right side please indicate first, how frequently you and the new teacher you mentored engaged in this activity; then, indicate how helpful you felt this activity was to the new teacher you mentored.

The new teacher I mentored and I engaged in this activity:
1 = never.
2 = one to several times per year.
3 = one to several times per month.
4 = one to several times per week.
5 = almost daily.

This activity was:
1 = not at all helpful to the new teacher.
2 = not very helpful to the new teacher.
3 = somewhat helpful to the new teacher.
4 = very helpful to the new teacher.
5 = extremely helpful to the new teacher.

Activity — I helped the new teacher I mentored:	Frequency: 1 Never	2 1–several times per year	3 1–several times per month	4 1–several times per week	5 Almost daily	Helpfulness: 1 Not at all helpful	2 Not very helpful	3 Somewhat helpful	4 Very helpful	5 Extremely helpful
1. By meeting in person in scheduled meetings.	1	2	3	4	5	1	2	3	4	5
2. By meeting in impromptu meetings (stopping by or meeting briefly in the hall).	1	2	3	4	5	1	2	3	4	5
3. By calling to check in.	1	2	3	4	5	1	2	3	4	5
4. By communicating in writing such as notes or email.	1	2	3	4	5	1	2	3	4	5
5. By observing his/her classroom & providing feedback.	1	2	3	4	5	1	2	3	4	5
6. Organize and manage his/her time.	1	2	3	4	5	1	2	3	4	5
7. Develop a classroom discipline plan.	1	2	3	4	5	1	2	3	4	5
8. Understand the district's teacher evaluation process.	1	2	3	4	5	1	2	3	4	5
9. Find materials & resources to use with the students.	1	2	3	4	5	1	2	3	4	5
10. Use a variety of teaching techniques with the students.	1	2	3	4	5	1	2	3	4	5
11. Deal with the stress of the job.	1	2	3	4	5	1	2	3	4	5
12. Understand the laws & regulations related to special education as implemented in the school district.	1	2	3	4	5	1	2	3	4	5
13. Administer & interpret standardized tests for program planning.	1	2	3	4	5	1	2	3	4	5
14. Develop curriculum in accordance with student needs and the state and district curriculum.	1	2	3	4	5	1	2	3	4	5
15. Learn the policies, procedures and routines of the school & district (such as discipline, attendance, etc.).	1	2	3	4	5	1	2	3	4	5
16. Plan a daily schedule.	1	2	3	4	5	1	2	3	4	5
17. Learn to prepare for and write IEPs according to district policy.	1	2	3	4	5	1	2	3	4	5
18. Work collaboratively with parents.	1	2	3	4	5	1	2	3	4	5
19. By providing emotional support when discouraged or frustrated	1	2	3	4	5	1	2	3	4	5
20. Develop daily and unit lesson plans.	1	2	3	4	5	1	2	3	4	5
21. By offering a variety of behavior management strategies to use with the students.	1	2	3	4	5	1	2	3	4	5
22. By providing support and encouragement.	1	2	3	4	5	1	2	3	4	5
23. Get to know & work with other school & district staff.	1	2	3	4	5	1	2	3	4	5
24. Get to know and work with the principal.	1	2	3	4	5	1	2	3	4	5

☐ Mentor's Self-Assessment (page 3 of 4)

Influence of Mentoring. The literature suggests that being a mentor teacher is a learning experience for both the mentor and the new teacher. Below, please answer the following questions related to your professional and personal performance as a function of being a mentor.

Being a mentor has:	Y = Yes N = No	If "Yes" to what extent do you believe this to be true? 1 = only a little true 2 = somewhat true 3 = moderately true 4 = very true 5 = extremely true				
1. made me a more effective teacher.	Y N	1	2	3	4	5
2. made me a more collaborative colleague.	Y N	1	2	3	4	5
3. increased my behavior management skills.	Y N	1	2	3	4	5
4. made me more effective pertaining to required special education paperwork.	Y N	1	2	3	4	5
5. made me more effective at time management.	Y N	1	2	3	4	5
6. made me a better leader.	Y N	1	2	3	4	5
7. made me a better model for effective teaching.	Y N	1	2	3	4	5
8. made me a more positive role model.	Y N	1	2	3	4	5
9. increased my commitment to the profession.	Y N	1	2	3	4	5
10. enabled me to deal with my own professional frustrations better.	Y N	1	2	3	4	5
11. increased my awareness of the district's practices and policies.	Y N	1	2	3	4	5
12. made me more respected by my peers.	Y N	1	2	3	4	5
13. made me more respected by my administrators.	Y N	1	2	3	4	5
14. increased my confidence in teaching different subject content.	Y N	1	2	3	4	5
15. increased my collaborative problem solving skills.	Y N	1	2	3	4	5
16. made me a more effective peer observer.	Y N	1	2	3	4	5
17. improved my skills as a consultant.	Y N	1	2	3	4	5
18. rejuvenated my interest in teaching.	Y N	1	2	3	4	5
19. increased my stress as a teacher.	Y N	1	2	3	4	5
20. a negative influence on the academic progress of my own students.	Y N	1	2	3	4	5
21. took me away from my own students too much.	Y N	1	2	3	4	5
22. created tension between me and other faculty.	Y N	1	2	3	4	5
23. created tension between me and the administration.	Y N	1	2	3	4	5
24. required too much of my time for too little compensation.	Y N	1	2	3	4	5

☐ Mentor's Self-Assessment (page 4 of 4)

Please answer the following questions as they relate to the building principal of your school. If there was more than one principal, please answer as they relate to the one most responsible for your mentoring activities and duties. If you were not assigned to one school, please answer as they relate to the administrator most responsible for your mentoring activities and duties.

1. How important do you feel building level administrative support is for successful mentoring?

   1   2   3   4   5

   Not At All Important   Not Very Important   Somewhat Important   Very Important   Extremely Important

2. How supportive was your building administrator in your mentoring efforts?

   1   2   3   4   5

   Not At All Supportive   Not Very Supportive   Somewhat Supportive   Very Supportive   Extremely Supportive

3. Did your building administrator provide release time for you to:

   Yes _____ No _____

   _____ _____ observe the new teacher you mentored? If so, how many times did you observe? _____

   _____ _____ conference with the new teacher you mentored? If so, how many times did you conference? _____

   _____ _____ attend planned training sessions? If so, how many training sessions did you attend? _____

4. Did your building administrator reduce your extra curricular duties while you were assigned to mentor a new teacher?

   Yes _____ No _____ Not applicable _____

   If "No", why not? _____

5. Did your building administrator reduce the extra curricular duties of the new teacher you mentored? Yes _____ No _____

   If "No", why not? _____

Please answer the following questions as they relate to any training you were provided this year.

6. Were you provided a formal training session(s) at the beginning of the year to help orient you to the mentoring program and your role and responsibilities as a mentor teacher? Yes _____ No _____

7. Were you provided formal training sessions throughout the year related to your needs as a mentor teacher? Yes _____ No _____

8. Were you provided training or debriefing sessions with just other mentors? Yes _____ No _____

   If "Yes" how helpful were those, or if "No" how helpful do you feel they could have been?

   1   2   3   4   5

   Not At All Helpful   Not Very Helpful   Somewhat Helpful   Very Helpful   Extremely Helpful

9. If you answered "Yes" to any of the above, please list the top five topics that were of greatest help to you during these training sessions.

10. What suggestions do you have to improve the training sessions or make them more relevant to your needs?

■ Chapter Five

The Mentoring Coordinator

The Circulatory System of a Mentoring Program

Learn About...

- ■ **Implementing a New Program**

- ■ **Developing Programs and Policies**

- ■ **Considerations**

- ■ **Collaboration and Commitment**

- ■ **Encouraging Mentors**

- ■ **Professional Development**

- ■ **Compensation and Release Time**

- ■ **Program Evaluation**

- ■ **Costs and Cost-Effectiveness**

- ■ **Issues**

The overall success of the program will rise and fall with the skills and influence of the mentoring coordinator. Coordinators circulate information and resources to new teachers, mentors, school personnel, district personnel, and state educational system personnel who work with and support the mentoring program. Coordinators are the lifeblood that keeps the support, information, and resources flowing effectively.

Coordinators have responsibility for guaranteeing the smooth and effective operation of the overall mentoring program. This includes ensuring that mentors have sufficient opportunities to mentor and the communication skills to guide new teachers.

Who is an appropriate choice to fill the role of mentoring program coordinator? While the qualifications of the coordinator are important, even more important is the quality of the coordination. The coordinating role can be filled by someone from any number of positions in the school district, including staff developers or supervisors of special education or elementary/secondary education. Larger districts will probably find that they need at least one administrator whose primary responsibilities relate to induction and mentoring. Often that person's main area of focus is elementary or secondary education. In some districts, mentoring may be coordinated by a specialist in elementary or secondary education with input and advice from the district director of special education. In smaller districts, the primary responsibility for special education mentor programs may rest with the director of special education.

Each of the approaches to coordinating has its own advantages and disadvantages. When programs are operated from an elementary program or secondary program base, there is greater assurance that information important for all new teachers will be shared with new special educators. This is critical under an inclusion model, where special educators and students with disabilities spend considerable time in general education classrooms. On the other hand, when special educator mentoring is coordinated from a base in special education, there is a higher likelihood that information specifically relevant to special educators—such as how to handle legal requirements and district special education policies—is part of the induction program.

Coordinators must consider how to involve others who are in roles critical to the mentoring induction program. Their involvement is necessary in order to further their commitment and support for the program. For example, the coordinator might establish a team to assist with the development of districtwide policies and procedures. Members of the team might include principals, experienced special education teachers, mentor teachers, faculty from teacher preparation programs, and new teachers—all of whom can provide valuable input into the plan.

Many districts have existing mentoring programs that are operated as part of the general induction program. Special education mentoring programs should be coordinated with these programs to ensure that each program complements the other.

District coordinators for the Mentoring Induction Project took different approaches to fulfilling their roles. Some worked closely with the general education mentoring coordinators who often had the ultimate responsibility for mentoring all new teachers in the district. Others were hired as part of the state's special education State Improvement Plan and had a close relationship with staff hired at the state level for these projects. Some of the coordinators spent considerable time collaborating with professors at nearby universities. In some cases, responsibilities for mentoring of new teachers in a district were shared with university staff.

■ Implementing a New Program

Today, it is likely that most new special education teachers participate in a districtwide mentoring program. Such involvement may encourage the needed dialogue between general and special educators. However, in a general program it is more difficult to take the unique needs and concerns of special educators into account.

Coordinators who are just starting a mentoring program or who are adding a special education component to their program may want to consider a pilot program—perhaps working with certain schools, grade levels, or types of special education programs. Pilot tests may provide the much needed opportunity to monitor implementation closely as policies are developed, materials are gathered, and funding for more widespread implementation is found. Pilot tests also can allow the coordinator to locate any obstacles to effective implementation and perhaps even to work through these to garner the necessary support and refine the program.

Expanding from Pilot to Comprehensive Districtwide Programs

Discussions with mentoring coordinators have confirmed the evolutionary nature of program implementation. Most districts begin to feel most confident about the nature and success of their mentoring components during the third year of implementation. It typically takes a couple of years to work out necessary adjustments. Two years often will provide everyone involved in the mentoring program the time to evaluate its impact. Even if the program involves simply adding a special education component, it is likely that it will take at least one year to refine the process.

■ Developing District Programs and Policies

Currently, many school districts have mentoring induction programs. However, the nature and effectiveness of these programs vary widely. Designers of many of these programs have not considered the unique nature of special education concerns.

The considerations and recommendations presented in this section can help to organize and prioritize the process of building a new program from the ground up or refining an existing program. A vital consideration is how the mentoring program will address the roles and responsibilities of the mentor and new teacher.

> *"When I feel like quitting, all it takes is to see my former beginning teachers smiling, teaching advanced courses, or heading up school committees ... and that gets me past the feeling."*
>
> **—Mentor
> (as quoted in Auton et al., 2002)**

Mentoring policies should be developed with adequate input and support from key stakeholders in the school district, including

- New special education teachers.
- Mentors.
- Staff developers.
- Directors of special education.
- Directors of elementary and secondary education.
- Human resources professionals responsible for recruitment and hiring.
- Other district level administrators.

Meeting with building level administrators can help to ensure their commitment to the program.

Collaboration with special education teacher preparation programs at nearby colleges and universities can be especially helpful. Networking with staff at state, regional, and federal mentoring induction programs and other professional development programs such as the Comprehensive System of Personnel Development (CSPD) also can be very helpful. Coordinators must consider the need for coordination with union representatives. Involving stakeholders such as these can not only help to ensure realistic and comprehensively planned policies, but also can help to ensure a strong flow of communication and support. For example, the Oregon Recruitment and Retention Project (2004) offers the following suggestions for special education administrators:

- Provide a special education orientation.
- Provide written materials such as a special education policy and procedures handbook.
- Clearly articulate and define roles and responsibilities.
- Institute a system to ensure communication.
- Make informal contact at least once per month (e.g., phone, email, in person).
- Establish a formal meeting schedule.
- Set up a schedule for conducting formal observations based on the district's evaluation policy.
- Provide clear feedback and specific suggestions for improvement.
- Clarify the educator's responsibility for attending special education staff meetings.
- Share resources and information targeted to beginning educators on an ongoing basis.
- Provide opportunities to visit other classrooms and network with other special education personnel.
- Support participation in professional organizations and associations.

Sometimes working with a local education association or a chapter of an organization such as the Council for

Exceptional Children can be useful. In some districts, mentoring programs are implemented by members of the CEC division for administrators, the Council for Administrators of Special Education. In other places, one way to involve the university may be to work through student CEC chapters or through CEC's Teacher Education Division.

■ Considerations When Developing a New Program or Improving an Existing One

A coordinator is necessary. Simply assigning a mentor to a new teacher is inadequate. The need for a coordinator cannot be overemphasized because mentoring involves release time, compensation, and negotiation. Someone needs to be the point person to manage these types of issues.

The best programs include some structured expectations, measurable criteria for success, and clearly defined activities. Some of the mixed results reported about the effectiveness of mentoring are a direct reflection of the lack of resources and management provided to support these aspects of the programs.

Mentor coordinators should compare the existing or proposed program (or program plan) to the Mentoring Induction Guidelines found in Chapter 2 of this book. They should locate areas of strength and deficiencies and collaborate with others as needed to refine the proposed program to meet specifications of these guidelines. The checklist in Chapter 2 can be used to review or develop the intended goals and impact of the proposed program.

Mentor coordinators should be familiar with state and district policies and practices. They should check to see what induction programs are in place, whether any special provisions have been made for special educators, and what the state and local requirements are for mentoring for all teachers—as well as any particular specifications for special educators. States sometimes will have different requirements for beginning teachers than for experienced teachers who are new to the

district. Some kind of mentoring, albeit modified and less intense, is recommended for teachers transferring into the district. In special education this is particularly important for incoming teachers who are assigned to grade levels or disability programs that differ from their prior experience or area of certification.

Mentor coordinators will want to check policies regarding second- and third-year teachers. Many districts require mentoring for these teachers. However, many districts have programs where mentoring gradually tapers off during the course of two to three years.

Mentor programs should address the specific concerns of special education teachers. Mentor coordinators should make sure that mentors have appropriate training in assisting new teachers. This includes pedagogy mastery, excellent communication skills, and knowledge of basic adult education principles. Mentors need to be able to establish trust and provide feedback in ways that support and guide new teachers through self-reflection.

Mentor coordinators may want to review materials in this guide and consider how recommendations, readings, or resources could be incorporated into mentor training activities. It may be helpful to talk with other administrators and researchers across the country who have implemented mentoring to find out about their successes and any difficulties they encountered.

Mentoring must be distinguished from performance evaluation. This must be made clear to all participants. Also, it is important to distinguish between mentoring of credentialed teachers and those with emergency credentials from alternative certification programs. The latter group will need more intensive mentoring.

For example, in Massachusetts, each school district is required to submit individual provisional educator program plans that include evidence of joint sponsorship or collaboration with colleges or universities, other districts, or other programs approved by the Commissioner of Education. Provisional educators must be observed and evaluated by a professional support team whose members have been trained by the department

☐ Areas of Focus for Mentor Coordinators When Developing a New Special Education Teacher Program

- Include structured expectations.

- Locate areas of strength and deficiencies and refine the program to meet specifications of guidelines.

- Be familiar with district policies and practices and programs from local universities or nearby districts.

- Establish a team to develop guidelines and policies.

- Address specific concerns of special educators.

- Incorporate recommendations, readings, and resources.

- Tap the experience and expertise of other mentor coordinators and researchers.

- Distinguish the mentoring process from program evaluation.

- Distinguish between mentoring of credentialed special educators and emergency-certified teachers.

- Set specific program policies regarding operation.

- Focus strongly on mentors and beginning teachers.

- Provide training.

- Provide time.

- Provide support.

of education. Minnesota and New Jersey have similar requirements. However, in Minnesota, the support team must include administrators, teachers, and postsecondary faculty members; in New Jersey, the team must include a building level administrator, a mentor, and one other person.

Decisions must be made regarding policies. Examples include use of substitutes; the scope of the program; professional development; and expectations regarding observations, conferencing, record keeping, and mentor compensation.

The program focus should be on the mentor and the beginning teacher. Both will require professional development and orientation. They will need time to attend inservice meetings and time for observation and conferencing. If possible, these teachers should be excused from at least some of the normal nonclassroom responsibilities (e.g., committee work, extracurricular responsibilities) so that they will have time to focus on professional development. Critical informal support often is provided through the incidental, unscheduled conversations that occur in the hallway, teachers' lounge, cafeteria, or library. Mentors and new teachers should be encouraged to take advantage of these opportunities to share questions and information.

■ *Establishing General Education and Special Education Collaboration and Commitment*

Some mentoring programs are designed specifically for special educators. In other programs, special educators may participate as a part of the districtwide mentoring program. There are advantages and disadvantages to each structure. Certainly, collaboration is important and ameliorates the isolation that many first-year special education teachers find to be a barrier to their development. On the other hand, mentoring that is designed for general educators may overlook some topics and approaches that are essential to special education such as how to handle paperwork, IEPs, assessment, scheduling, serious discipline concerns, and instruction with low-incidence populations.

When developing and implementing the mentor program, it helps to have input from staff developers, directors of special education, directors of elementary and secondary education, human resource office staff, building administrators, participating university or college faculty, and, in some cases, union officials. Throughout the implementation phase, the mentoring coordinator must maintain close communication not only with mentors and new teachers, but also with building level administrators so that their issues and concerns are handled appropriately. Success in program design and implementation requires sensitivity to the demands of other ongoing district priorities.

Collaboration with Nearby Teacher Preparation Programs

Collaboration with nearby teacher preparation programs is advantageous for several reasons. These include:

- It will assist university faculty in better understanding the needs of new teachers and should, with time, increase the effectiveness of their preservice programs.

- University faculty may have valuable research knowledge, materials, or information concerning funding sources.

- University faculty may have expertise to assist with the inservice training for mentors and new teachers.

Boyer and Gillespie (2000) examined a variety of options used by mentoring programs for supporting teachers. Brief descriptions of several of these options follow.

- The Oregon Recruitment/Retention Project, a state funded program, works directly with local school districts to help design mentor programs (**http://www.tr.wou.edu/rrp/index.htm**). Administrators whose districts are in need of support may consider approaching their state departments of education to request similar legislation.

- The College of Education in Southwest Texas (**http://www.utsa.edu/gcat/chapter7/coehd/**

dsltdept.cfm#mamasec) offers a master's program in special education that sends nontraditional students into the classroom as paid interns for their second year and provides full-time mentoring support as part of on-the-job training. Districts may find that their local universities are an untapped source of mentoring expertise. While the Mentoring Induction Project did not address how to mentor those in alternative certification programs, there is a tremendous need for mentoring of these teachers, and more information is needed to better understand how to implement mentors for these new teachers who have not been enrolled in a traditional university preparation program.

- The Fairfax County Public Schools, Virginia, include special education teachers in a 17-session, year-long course designed for general classroom teachers. This training addresses the issue of inclusiveness that many special education teachers describe to us as their main challenge. The course, entitled "Beginning Teacher Induction Program," also includes a mentoring component and optional courses for teachers whose students have special needs. More information on that program, including sample forms, can be found at **www.fcps.k12.va.us/index.shtml**.

Ensuring the Commitment of Building Administrators

The most successful mentoring programs are ones where building administrators understand the importance of mentoring and are supportive of the needs and concerns of both new teachers and mentors. Both mentors and new teachers stress the importance of support from the building administrator.

It is important for the mentoring program coordinator to involve principals in the design of the mentoring program and to communicate mentoring expectations and needs to principals. This does not mean that each principal is involved, but rather that there is input from two or three representative principals. Coordinators also should be aware of administrator concerns regarding unique needs in particular schools (such as unique population served, difficulties locating substitute teachers, stresses related to high-stakes assessment, or past difficulties that may have occurred in implementing mentoring).

Building administrators typically are involved in the nomination of master teachers to serve as mentors. Principals and other building administrators also can support mentoring programs by ensuring that release time is available to the new teacher and mentor, reducing the teaching load or extracurricular responsibilities for the new teacher and mentor, and encouraging the mentor and new teacher to meet regularly.

In communicating with principals and other building level administrators, the mentor coordinator must consider ways to increase his or her knowledge of and sensitivity to the needs and responsibilities of first-year teachers. This is particularly important in light of several studies that cite lack of administrative support as one of the most important determinants of a teacher's decision to stop teaching special education (Billingsley & Cross, 1991; Kozleski et al., 2001).

■ *Encouraging Mentors*

With the current pressure on schools to make AYP, mentors may find that new teachers are expected to achieve significant student improvements, teach to standards, and establish effective discipline plans. This does not change the likelihood that some teachers will simply be ineffective or will be a poor match for the teaching situation. The coordinator will want to build a relationship with mentors that will provide a platform for investigating how to handle each of these issues. Sometimes it is simply a matter of one other person, such as the coordinator, observing and providing feedback to a new teacher that is similar to the feedback provided by the mentor. At other times, a visit by a coordinator may help a new teacher by providing input from a different perspective. In any event, the coordinator will be most effective as he or she encourages the new teacher and mentor to continue to solve problems.

At times, the coordinator also may need to help the mentor set boundaries with the administrator so that it is clearly understood that the mentor cannot be effective if she or he also is evaluating the new teacher. Often, the mentor will be a source of collegial support after a performance evaluation has been conducted by the school administrator. The combined impact of the formal evaluation and the informal supports from the mentor provide a strong catalyst for improvement.

■ *Developing and Providing Inservice Training Sessions and Materials*

A successful mentoring program depends in part on the training and development provided. In providing inservice training for mentors and new teachers, the coordinator will need to develop materials to support the program, including background articles for new teachers and mentors, district requirements for IEPs and paperwork, and a written description of district expectations for mentors and new teachers.

When the coordinator prepares a training program, the basic requirements and organization of the program must be considered. Examples include:

- Number of contact hours (generally at least 60-90 hours between mentor and new teacher during the first year of teaching).

- Record keeping (contact logs).

- Needs assessments and action plans.

- Inservice training and other professional development opportunities.

- Policies regarding confidentiality.

- Expectations regarding procedures to follow when difficulties arise.

- How to address lack of administrative support if that is the case.

- How to proceed if mentors are not receiving time to observe and coach new teachers or other mentoring guidelines are not being followed.

- Incentives that will be used to encourage participation and follow through.

- How to organize and deliver support to second and third-year teachers.

In designing a program, the coordinator also will want to carefully review the:

- Characteristics of the population.

- Expectations and culture of the city, town, or rural area.

☐ Training Topics for Mentors

According to mentors participating in the Mentoring Induction Program project, mentor teacher training topics should include but not be limited to:

- Roles and expectations of the mentor.

- Needs of new teachers and their roles and responsibilities in the mentoring process.

- Effective communication skill development incorporating adult education principles.

- Consultation strategies, including how to give constructive feedback and social support.

- Time management and organizational strategies.

- Classroom observation skills.

- Updates on IEP development and implementation changes, special education laws, and paperwork requirements.

- Advising and coaching skills.

- Behavior management strategies across grade levels and disabilities.

- Collaboration and problem-solving skills.

- Curriculum and instructional strategies.

- Successes and problems of any ongoing programs.

Some background research or consultation sometimes may be necessary so that the mentoring program builds on a success-oriented model. This may mean collaboration with other projects that will focus on program improvement.

Orientation

Both mentors and beginning teachers need orientation sessions prior to the beginning of the school year. This will provide an opportunity to introduce the new teacher to the district and the school and to gain an understanding of the framework, expectations, and timeline for mentoring activities.

Mentor Training

Mentors often are selected on the basis of their accomplishments with students, but they are evaluated for effectiveness as a mentor on the accomplishments of the beginning teacher with whom they work (Little, 1990). For that reason, mentors must be trained in a systematic way to become mentors.

Different mentor training programs are available in different states, and the characteristics of the teachers and school system are the primary criteria for choosing an appropriate program. As program developers evaluate program models, they also must consider the unique needs of special educators. If a training program does not accommodate these needs, they must incorporate specific components that address them. Once a system has been adopted, training for mentors should begin prior to the school year and before they are assigned a new teacher. And, it must continue throughout the year.

The North Carolina State Department of Public Instruction (1997) listed the following topics as appropriate for mentor training:

- Rationale for induction support.

- Characteristics of novice teachers.

- Skills for identifying needs and concerns of novice teachers.

- Building a helping relationship.

- Adult development and learning theory.

- Role and function of mentor teachers.

- Cognitive coaching and interactive problem solving.

- Classroom observation and conferencing skills.

- Strategies for facilitating teacher reflection.

- Assessment methodology and instrumentation.

- Understanding the state licensing program.

The agency also recommends using high-quality principles of professional development when designing mentor training. These principles include:

- Using content based on the research literature.

- Providing opportunities to practice skills with feedback.

- Providing opportunities to apply concepts to simulated situations.

- Assessing participant mastery of concepts.

- Scheduling follow-up sessions for participants to debrief experiences.

☐ Timelines and Benchmarks

Fall	Winter	Spring	Summer
September ■ Conduct needs assessments ■ Develop action plans		**March–April** ■ Solicit mentor nominations ■ Select mentors	**July–August** ■ Provide mentor-new teacher training
September–May ■ Mentors conduct observations and provide feedback **October-May** ■ Provide additional inservice for mentors and new teachers			**August** ■ Match mentors and new teachers
		April-May ■ Evaluate program ■ Plan revisions for next year	**August–September** ■ Provide orientation ■ Communicate expectations to principals for current program year

■ Assessing the effectiveness of mentor's performance with beginning teachers.

Mentor training also may need to address unique program needs. This is especially true when a new teacher is involved in a specialty program. Examples include:

■ Early childhood programs that include home visits.

■ Transition-to-work programs that involve collaboration with the business community.

■ Center-based programs for students with emotional/behavioral problems.

■ Programs serving students with autism.

New Teacher Professional Development

Staff development activities for new teachers should span the course of the academic school year. Development programs should include the areas identified by new special educators as areas in which they most often need help. In one survey, paperwork, IEPs, parent conferencing, job stressors, using the general curriculum, referral and placement/reevaluation, behavior management, and assessment were the highest rated items (White & Mason, 2002). For more training topics for new teachers, see Chapter 3.

Setting Timelines and Benchmarks

It is important to plan ahead to consider timing for orientations to the mentoring program. These orientations should occur prior to or during the first few weeks of school. Timing of inservice training also should be built into districtwide inservice schedules.

Provisions for release time for observations and conferencing must be made. The district may wish to follow the procedure used in Granite School District (Salt Lake City, Utah), where a cadre of paraeducators was prepared to deliver specific lessons to students on topics such as social skills development and to substitute for the new teachers or mentors as needed. Some of the major benchmarks and suggested timelines are outlined in the text box, *Timelines and Benchmarks*.

■ *Arranging Compensation and Release Time*

The importance of adequate release time for mentors and new teachers cannot be stressed enough. It is essential to the success of the mentoring program. The coordinator arranges for compensation and release time for mentors and new teachers to cover inservice professional development, observations, and conferencing.

In addition to release time, mentors should receive some sort of compensation. This may include stipends, tuition waivers, professional development opportunities, a reduced teaching load, or other forms of professional recognition. Data from a 50-state review conducted by the American Federation of Teachers (2001) were very similar to more recent data from Learning Point Associates (2004). The AFT report showed that

■ Thirty-three states have induction policies, and 29 require that mentors are assigned to beginning teachers; however, only 22 states mandate and fund these programs, and 60 percent of these states specify exemptions (often for teachers on emergency certification).

■ Twelve states require that mentors receive stipends (generally $500 to $1,000 per year), 17 states require that mentors receive training, and 21 have established criteria for mentors.

■ Only two states (Kentucky and New York) require mentors to have reduced teaching loads.

■ *Documenting and Evaluating the Program*

In addition to providing inservice training, release time, and compensation to new teachers and their mentors, the mentoring program coordinator is responsible for developing forms and other documentation necessary to run the program. A variety of forms from the district may be helpful in developing mentoring programs. Forms and protocols that may need to be developed include:

■ Forms for nominating and selecting mentors.

■ Action plans for mentors and new teachers.

- Observation protocols and forms.
- Forms for recording conferences between mentors and new teachers.
- Logs for recording participation.
- Forms for requesting mentor compensation.

Most important, the coordinator should develop protocols for assessing the effectiveness of the mentoring program. These can include both formal and informal methods. For example, a structured interview of new teachers may include questions and prompts such as the following:

- Describe the types of problems with which you received assistance during the past year.
- Describe the types of suggestions you were given during the past year.
- How much time did your mentor spend with you during the past year?
- Was the assistance provided to you adequate?
- Was the assistance valuable to you? In what ways?
- What suggestions do you have for improving the mentor program?

The University of California at Irvine (Peterson, 2002) suggests gathering feedback throughout the year that describes the mentor program. This may include formal surveys and structured interviews. In addition, background information might be gathered that includes:

- Number of participants.
- Overview of the training and services provided.
- The resources required to operate the program.

The text box, *Feedback and Recommendations*, shows a tool developed by the Akron (Ohio) Public Schools for assessing its mentor program.

Mentoring may take place in a hub of activity, in the classroom, or in meetings that are sandwiched between other responsibilities. Because of the nature of the school day and other demands on their schedules, mentors, teachers, and administrators may not take time to document the progress of the program. Evaluations and assessments, however, are critical for the maintenance of a long-term mentoring program. Taking the time to document and assess the reflections, observations, and suggestions from all participants will help lay the foundation for a successful mentor program for years to come.

■ *Understanding the Costs and Cost Effectiveness of Mentoring*

The mentoring coordinator or administrator will need to estimate costs. In an online survey of 110 school districts, 21 percent indicated that they had mentoring programs and provided information on costs and funding (Mason & O'Connell, 2002). While the data that follow should be viewed as preliminary due to the small sample size (n=23 districts) and wide variations in the demographics for these districts, they may be useful, particularly when compared to other existing data. Findings include:

- The districts hired an average of 33 new special education teachers at an average recruitment and hiring cost of $2,397 per teacher.
- These districts estimated the cost for induction for each new teacher to be an average of $735, and reported an increase in induction expenses over three years.
- Mentoring programs had been in effect a mean of 4.38 years.
- The districts reported a mean of 36 mentors in 2001-2002 at an average cost per mentor of $835 for the overall mentoring program.
- The districts reported a mean of 12 special education mentors at an average cost of $354 per special education mentor.
- Funding for special education mentoring in the 23 districts came largely from local education agencies. However, state education agencies, federal projects, general education, and private foundation funds also were valuable sources of funding.

☐ Feedback and Recommendations

1) Mentor Criteria: Rank the following criteria for selecting a mentor for a new teacher, with 1 being the most important and 5 being the least important. A mentor should:

_____ Be in the same building.

_____ Teach the same disability area.

_____ Teach the same grade range.

_____ Have at least three years of teaching experience.

_____ Be nominated by the principal.

2) Contact Time: How much time per month should a mentor and a new teacher spend with each other?

3) Time for Activities: Break down the time you listed for Question 2 and indicate how much time should be spent, per month, on the following types of contact:

_____ Face to face.   _____ Telephone.

_____ Email.   _____ Notes.

4) Value of substitute days: If you took a sub day, how meaningful was it on a scale of 1 to 5, with 1 being "highly meaningful"?

_____ Number of sub days.

_____ Meaningful?

5) How many sub days should each new teacher have per year?

6) Sub day activities: List five meaningful activities that new teachers could do during a sub day.

7) Value of new teacher professional development series: How meaningful was it on a scale of 1 to 5, with 1 being "highly meaningful"?

8) New teacher professional development series format: What would be the ultimate format for the new teacher series? Include:

_____ Number of sessions?

_____ When they are offered through the year (one per month or more frequent in the fall)?

_____ Day and time of sessions (how many hours)?

_____ One topic per session or continue the "menu" format?

_____ Have all participants together or split up by age level or by disability area served?

9) New teacher professional development series topics: List five of the most important topics to cover in the series.

10) Mentor training format: What would be the ultimate format for training mentors? Include:

_____ Number of sessions?

_____ When they are offered through the year (one per month or more frequent in the fall)?

_____ Day and time of sessions (how many hours)?

_____ One topic per session or continue the "menu" format?

11) Mentor training topics: List five of the most important topics to cover for mentors.

12) What other recommendations do you have for mentoring first-year teachers? What else would make the first year better?

Reference: Akron Public Schools (2002).

While data on the costs of providing mentoring for special educators are difficult to locate, cost data for general education mentoring programs show costs to be between $1,200 and $5,000 per teacher. Estimates in Texas included $500 for the mentor stipend, $300 for training support team members, $450 for release days for the new teacher and mentor, and $75 for program coordination. In comparison, Rochester, New York, reported spending $5,000, and Illinois reported spending up to $16,000 per new teacher for mentoring (Black, 2001; Illinois State Board of Education, 2000).

To put this in perspective, costs for overall professional development typically were estimated to range from 1.8 percent to three percent of the district's total budget—reported to be between $1,000 and $16,000 per teacher, suggesting that costs per teacher for mentoring, at least in some districts, may be equivalent to professional development expenses (Miles et al., 2002; Miller, Lord, & Dorney, 1994).

Cost Effectiveness Considerations

Findings in the districts responding to the Mason and O'Connell (2002) survey, with the data reported in terms of averages across the 23 districts, included:

- The mean number of new teachers hired decreased from 40 to 33.

- Recruitment and hiring costs increased from $1,445 to $2,397 per new teacher.

- Induction costs increased from $689 to $735 per teacher.

- Sixty-five percent of the districts indicated that induction programs have improved, serving more teachers or providing more services.

For comparison purposes, available data on general recruitment-replacement costs for educators ranged from $5,000 to $50,000 (Villani, 2002). Several researchers have used a model employed in business to estimate the costs of replacing an individual teacher: A conservative model estimates these costs at between 25 percent and 35 percent of the annual salary plus the costs of fringe benefits. However, others have calculat-

ed costs at between 50 percent and 200 percent of the departing teacher's annual salary (Bliss, 2000; Ettorre, 1997; Fitzenz, 1997). These latter estimates are based on industry standards that consider not only recruitment and personnel expenditures, but also lost productivity (Wong & Wong, 2002). Hauenstein (1999) is among those who have developed formulas for calculating replacement costs. His formula includes such factors as termination costs, vacancy costs, hiring costs, learning curve costs, and training costs.

How to Budget

The mentoring budget should include funds for a mentoring program coordinator in each district. Districts should provide stipends or other compensation for mentors, and mentors as well as new teachers should be provided with training. Release time should be available for observations and conferences. Each of these factors should be built into the mentoring budget, along with funds for materials and resources to ensure that building level administrators are adequately informed of and involved with the mentoring program.

The size of the budget should be estimated based on attrition and vacancies in recent years. Coordinators also may find that all or part of the budget for mentoring is absorbed under general professional development and induction expenses, so careful coordination with other administrators who handle these areas may be essential.

Where possible, budget for mentoring as a separate line item in a district's budget, rather than combining these costs with general staff development expenses. Tracking mentoring costs separately will provide a framework for later comparing the costs of mentoring to recruitment, hiring, and other attrition-related expenses.

Why Mentoring Is Worth the Expense

Studies in both general and special education have indicated that teacher attrition is reduced with the introduction of mentoring. Other studies have demonstrated that self-confidence and teaching skills are enhanced when beginning teachers have mentoring supports. While more definitive data are needed on mentoring cost effectiveness, in general it appears that the dollars spent up front in orienting new teachers to the district and school and providing individualized mentoring supports will save districts time and dollars in recruitment, hiring, and orientation of additional new teachers.

Moreover, as was discovered in the Mentoring Induction Project, beginning teachers needed mentoring on paperwork, IEPs, and managing classroom behaviors—three activities that ate into instructional time. Teachers who choose to remain in their districts are familiar with district procedures and policies and have established behavioral support programs. Thus, these teachers are likely to spend more time focusing on instruction and student achievement.

■ *Issues That Mentoring Coordinators Face*

In facilitating the implementation of mentoring programs in seven districts across the United States, Mentoring Induction Project coordinators talked via phone conferences and at national meetings to solve problems and share ideas about implementation. Some of the situations they addressed:

- Coordinating special education mentoring with district and state requirements or expectations for involvement of special educators in more general mentoring programs.

- Garnering the support of building level administrators, who often were involved with myriad concerns.

- Matching mentors with new teachers.

- Funding release time for teacher observation.

- Coordinating mentoring activities with nearby colleges and universities.

Potential solutions to these challenges include:

- Involve general education administrators—including district level supervisors, curriculum specialists, and persons responsible for district level mentoring programs in the early planning stages.

- If possible, bring resources—including funding, which is sometimes available through state technical assistance programs—into the equation rather than expecting existing programs to fund special mentoring concerns.

- Consider not only what new special educators need to be successful, but also the training and activities that will enhance the knowledge and skills of new general education teachers to work with students with disabilities.

■ *In Summary—Planning Steps*

The mentor coordinator must consider the needs and concerns of many audiences (administrators at the building and district level, new teachers, and mentors) in designing and implementing a mentor program for special educators. Time spent up front in researching, designing a program, and obtaining buy-in from key stakeholders will provide many dividends during the implementation phase. Similarly, by using a variety of evaluative tools, the coordinator will obtain valuable information for refining the approach, increasing the satisfaction of participants, and strengthening the program. The text box, *To Do List for the Mentor Coordinator*, summarizes the recommended planning stages and activities.

☐ To Do List for the Mentor Coordinator

Conduct review of programs in other localities.

☐ Review national research.

☐ Conduct online searches.

Describe status quo in the district.

☐ Investigate whether special education teachers have been considered and if so, whether their needs are being met.

☐ Identify the strengths and weaknesses of the current program.

☐ Use the mentor induction program checklist in Chapter 2 to assess the program.

Solicit input.

☐ Discuss possibilities with leaders, administrators, teachers, and new teachers.

☐ Begin designing the program. Prepare proposal.

Prepare budget.

☐ Make sure funds are allocated and are sufficient.

☐ Determine if the program will be districtwide.

☐ Decide if a pilot program will be initiated first.

☐ Consider additional funding opportunities (e.g., State Improvement Grant monies, etc.).

Develop a summary of findings.

☐ Prepare an executive summary.

☐ Share findings with all stakeholders.

Form an advisory group if one does not already exist.

☐ Invite stakeholders to participate.

☐ Invite representatives from outside the district (e.g., teacher education faculty, etc.) to participate.

Meet with key stakeholders.

☐ Share proposal.

☐ Gather feedback.

Finalize proposal.

☐ Include key features, budget, and timeline for implementation.

☐ Get approval from district.

Implement the program.

☐ Advertise the program.

☐ Note areas of concern as well as areas of support.

☐ Determine mechanism for soliciting ongoing feedback.

Assess program effectiveness.

☐ Consider using interviews and focus groups during the first year.

☐ Conduct mid-year and end-of-year evaluations before planning for the second year.

■ Chapter Six

The Principal's Role

Providing Oxygen to Support the Mentoring Program*

Learn About...

■ **Role and Expectations of Principals**

■ **General Support**

■ **Mentor-New Teacher Match**

■ **Time**

■ **School-Related Information**

■ **Professional Development**

*Joan Wheeler co-authored this chapter.

The principal's understanding of the needs of special educators and students with disabilities gives a vital breath of life to an effective special education program. A principal who understands IDEA legislative requirements will be in a better position to support new teachers, mentor teachers, and the collaboration necessary between general and special educators. New teachers cannot possibly learn everything that is needed to be effective within the standard four years of teacher training provided by their college education. They need additional foundational support as they learn to apply the academic knowledge they have gathered.

As effective advocates for all students in the school, including students with disabilities, principals guide professional development activities. This includes demonstrating leadership in understanding and fostering strong mentoring relationships. Administrators support mentoring programs by:

■ Recognizing and building on the capabilities of the staff.

■ Planning for and supporting new teachers and their mentors as they engage in professional development.

Just as oxygen is delivered through the circulatory system, principals must work closely with the mentoring coordinator to facilitate professional development and inservice support.

■ *The Role and Expectations of Principals in the Mentoring Program*

Principals can support the mentoring program in their schools by working closely with the mentor coordinator. They also can advocate for and support mentoring programs within the school district.

Principals nominate and select experienced and talented teachers to be mentors and promote positive relationships between mentors and new teachers. They also are responsible for facilitating release time for observation and conferencing. Principals need to remain sensitive to situations that may be troublesome for new teachers as they acclimate to their new roles and to the culture of the particular school.

The benefits of having a mentor induction program for beginning special educators will reach beyond the beginning teacher and mentor to impact the entire school community. Principals can do several things to help make the new teacher's first year a smooth one, and a mentor induction program is a good place to begin. Although a principal can support the mentoring process in a variety of ways, research suggests the following areas of focus:

- General support.
- The mentor-new teacher match.
- Time.
- School-related information.
- Professional development.

Each will be discussed in the following sections.

■ General Support

A principal can be an energizing breath of fresh air to a new teacher. Beginning teachers, and particularly beginning special educators, report feeling isolated. Lack of support from administrators appears to contribute to the sense of isolation experienced by these new teachers. In fact, one of the reasons most frequently mentioned for beginning teachers leaving special education is a perceived lack of support from administrators (Whitaker, 2000). With a little effort and direction, principals can help beginning special educators feel comfortable in their new positions in the school.

Some activities suggested by the Oregon Recruitment and Retention Project (2004) for providing support follow:

- Provide a building orientation meeting.
- Assign an experienced general education staff member as a building guide.
- Make informal contact with the new teacher at least once per month (e.g., phone conversation, email, in person).
- Schedule quarterly meetings beginning with the orientation meeting.
- Clarify the beginning teacher's responsibility for attending staff meetings.
- Ensure written building policies and procedures have been provided.
- Provide opportunities for the new teacher to visit other classrooms and to network with teachers.

"My principal is wonderful, he's been really supportive as far as coming in and observing and giving feedback as well. It's just been kind of nice to have that support. He's also come in and, I was observing one time and [he] actually ended up getting involved in the lesson and ended up modeling the rest of the lesson for the students, which was nice because it reflected how important it was to the principal."

**—New Teacher
Mentoring Induction Project**

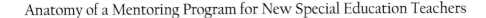

Open Communication

Principals can help to reduce new teacher feelings of isolation in several ways. First, beginning special education teachers prefer principals with an open style of communication (Brock & Grady, 1998). Communication is like breathing in and breathing out—it should be unobstructed. For example, a principal can engage in collegial conversations about the new teacher's work and encourage related professional growth and development (Hope, 1999).

Principals also should maintain an awareness of the school and classroom experiences of beginning teachers by stopping by the classroom to show confidence and support. This helps to establish a healthier, less hierarchical relationship and creates closer involvement with the staff and students. Principals can show an interest during noninstructional times as well, such as in the hallway, the cafeteria, or during recess activities (Bartholomay, Wallace, & Mason, 2001).

The airways of communication also may be kept open in several other ways. Written information, such as email or weekly newsletters, is effective in informing teachers about school occurrences, activities, and events. Newsletters and emails also provide a place to recognize an individual teacher's accomplishments, highlighting the background, experience, or special skills of new teachers to help include them on the school team. In a more personal venue, principals may have group meetings or an informal monthly coffee with beginning teachers to encourage a more open, vital, and relaxed atmosphere.

Observations

While observations by administrators are not a part of the mentoring program, they are expected and valuable, and they certainly affect new teachers. As these observations occur, principals must take care that they remain separate from the mentoring process. In respect for the confidentiality and integrity of the mentoring process, mentors should not be expected to report observations or improvements to administrators. While mentors and new teachers may discuss principals' observations, and mentors may help new teachers prepare for these observations, it should be clear to all that these are two separate procedures.

That being said, the involvement of administrators is vital to special educators, and their feedback is valued. New teachers are often nervous during principals' initial visits to the classroom, and it helps if principals provide feedback in a timely manner and are encouraging and positive. Principals should focus on one area of need at a time and be sensitive to the teacher's need to "find his or her own way." As the year proceeds, they may wish to stop by and casually check in to offer guidance and support.

Consultations

After an observation there are several ways principals can show support to beginning teachers. They can offer personal assistance or ask another special education teacher to lend support, following through to see that the assistance is provided (Whitaker, 2000). If special education is not the principal's specialty, consultation with a curriculum specialist or district specialist is advised.

The principal can ensure that the beginning special educator is provided specialized assistance with instructional strategies. The principal may have resources available to send the beginning teacher to an inservice training session or suggest specific web sites. Lending a teacher books, handouts, or videos that address a specific area of need also may be helpful. In order not to overwhelm or smother the beginning teacher, the administrator should choose among these options and offer only one or two suggestions at a time.

Support in the School

Another way principals can support beginning teachers is to include them on the school team. They need to be introduced to other faculty and staff in the school, and a principal's show of faith can help them to become respected members of the faculty (Whitaker, 2000). The principal who sets a positive, enthusiastic, and supportive example goes a long way to setting the tone and expectations for the rest of the school. Throughout the school, the well-oxygenated muscle of a strong staff can perform better and sustain performance longer.

Support with Parents

Principals can take steps to ensure that beginning teachers develop successful relationships with parents and students. For example, because new special educa-

---

□ **Advantages for Principals Participating in a Mentor Induction Program**

- Increased retention rates for new teachers.

- Renewed practice for veteran teachers.

- A growing sense of professionalism in the school.

- Improved relationships with parents.

- A greater sense of community among teachers in the school.

- Expanded leadership roles of teachers in the school.

---

tors often are intimidated by their students' parents, it can help if the principal can be available as needed to assist with meetings (Whitaker, 2000). A principal can demonstrate support for the beginning teacher by becoming an active and informed team member in an IEP meeting. Prior to a child's IEP meeting, the principal must be sure to visit the classroom and become acquainted with the student. Although at times it will be necessary to send an administrative designee to an IEP meeting, it is recommended that this be the exception rather than the usual practice. Principals benefit from being aware of how the IEPs are implemented in the school and from maintaining contact with families, teachers, and students.

■ *The Mentor-New Teacher Match*

Principals typically assist with the nomination and selection of mentors. Assigning a mentor to a beginning teacher is a challenging yet necessary task. According to respondents to the Recruiting New Teachers study (1999), there is a 93 percent retention rate for teachers who participate in new teacher mentoring and training programs (Hillebrand, 1999). Recruitment and hiring of new teachers is a time consuming and expensive process. The effort put forth to retain beginning teachers through an effective mentoring program will be worthwhile in the long run, benefiting the school community by establishing a stable staff. With stability, it is easier for everyone involved to put their efforts toward school improvement goals (Hope, 1999).

Qualities of a Mentor

When making an appropriate match, administrators should consider the most desirable qualities of a mentor. Examples include the following considerations:

- The best mentors for special education teachers are teachers who teach special education themselves. The expectation is that special educators will mentor other special educators.

- Strong preference is given to teachers who teach in the same building and for teachers who teach students with similar disabilities (White & Mason, 2002).

- Mentors are teachers who are master teachers with at least three to five years of experience, and are knowledgeable and capable of providing instructional and emotional support (Brock & Grady, 1998; Rowley, 1999).

- Good mentors have strong interpersonal skills and credibility with their peers and administrators (Scherer, 1999). Communication skills are important characteristics that enable mentors to work effectively with beginning teachers (Scherer, 1999).

- Mentors need time, energy, and enthusiasm to work with beginning teachers, as well as curiosity and an eagerness to further their own knowledge (Scherer, 1999).

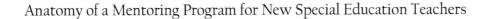
- Mentors who volunteer for the opportunity to work with beginning teachers are most successful (White & Mason, 2002).

More information on desirable qualities of a mentor is provided in Chapter 4.

School and Special Education Considerations

Requirements of a special education teacher can be very different from those of a general education teacher. This may make the principal's task of making the appropriate mentor-mentee match more challenging.

Several factors need to be considered when making this match. When all conditions cannot be met, White and Mason (2002) recommend that the following factors be considered in the order in which they are presented:

- Beginning special educators prefer to have mentors who teach special education.

- The mentor should teach in the same building as the beginning teacher, if at all possible. This facilitates the frequency and types of interactions that occur and makes support more easily accessible.

- The mentor should have experience teaching students with the same types of disabilities.

- It is useful to have mentors who have experience teaching students of the same age or grade levels.

Training for the Mentor

The likelihood of success is greater if mentors know what is expected of them and understand the needs of beginning teachers (Whitaker, 2000). According to Evertson and Smithey (2000), beginning teachers who have worked with trained mentors manage instruction more effectively and establish routines that are more workable than those whose mentors have had no training. Training also provides the opportunity to reflect and engage in problem solving with other mentors and to discover common needs among the beginning teachers. It is the principal's responsibility to provide the mentor with release time to attend these sessions.

Mentors as Supporters

Principals should keep in mind that the nature of the relationship between the mentor and the mentee is one of support. A mentor is not an evaluator, but instead accepts the beginning teacher and recognizes that his or her journey has just begun. When the beginning teacher struggles, the mentor provides meaningful support (Rowley, 1999). Some areas of support may include scheduling; planning; curriculum and instruction; discipline; time management; assistance with policies, procedures, and forms; or acting as a sounding board and source of encouragement (Whitaker, 2000).

Mentors as School Leaders

Mentors need support. Proactive and responsive professional development is an essential factor associated with school success (Bartholomay, Wallace, & Mason, 2001). Principals must pay close attention to the success of the mentor to recognize emerging leadership skills. Consider involving the mentor in future professional development activities for the mentoring program, or encourage the mentor to write an article regarding the mentoring experience. In an environment where you nurture innovations and provide practical knowledge, teachers may become agents for positive change in the school.

Benefits to Mentors

There are many positive outcomes of mentoring for the mentor. Mentors gain new perspectives on teaching and a greater sense of professionalism and collegiality. Their leadership skills improve and their self-esteem increases. Beginning teachers often bring new perspectives on current information in research, practices, and technology to the mentor, which enhances the mentor's instruction (Johnson & Kardos, 2002). It is exciting to see the growth and development of the beginning teacher and it may give the mentor satisfaction in the joy of giving (Fideler & Haselkorn, 1999). These benefits help to encourage veteran teacher participation in a mentoring program.

Incentives for Mentors

Incentives for mentors add to the benefit of their participation in a mentoring program. Providing stipends, continuing education credits (CEUs), release time, or tuition assistance formalizes the program, gives it credibility, and communicates to all participants that the program is valued (Scherer, 1999). A mentee feels more comfortable calling upon a mentor when he or she sees the value placed on the program by the mentor, the administration, and the district. Other possible incentives are extra planning time, limited extracurricular activities, or extra money to purchase materials. Like the pulmonary system and the circulatory system working in harmony, the principal and the mentoring coordinator need to work closely to plan and support the availability of such incentives.

An Unsuccessful Match

If a mentor-mentee match is not working, there are several options. A good first step is to talk with each of the team members to determine where the breakdown lies. Ensure that the mentor has the training to support the beginning teacher in a way that is helpful and effective.

Examine the personality styles involved. If all else fails, the beginning teacher may need to be reassigned to a different mentor. If it is well into the school year, the principal must determine whether the beginning teacher has formed an informal mentoring relationship with a different teacher in the school. Communicate your concerns with the mentoring coordinator to seek assistance about how to proceed.

■ *Time*

Research indicates that a good match between mentor and beginning teacher is crucial, and that the most important thing a principal can do to benefit the mentoring process is to provide the mentor and mentee with plenty of time (Hope, 1999; Holloway, 2001; Johnson & Kardos, 2002; Whitaker, 2000). In planning for release time and scheduling, principals will need to work closely with the mentor program coordinator to ensure

that they have considered the mentoring plan as it will be implemented in their district.

Mentors and new teachers need time for the following activities:

- **Time to plan**. Beginning teachers report that emotional support is their greatest need in working with their mentor, and they need time to build a relationship to gain that emotional support. Mentors often discover that participation in professional development for an induction program improves their own teaching skills and engages them in reflection about their own instructional practices (Holloway, 2001). When the two have ample time to meet, they plan lessons and specify goals and objectives, procedures, and anticipated outcomes for an upcoming lesson. Upon reviewing the lesson at a later meeting, the teacher will have an opportunity to reflect on the plan, its implementation, and outcomes for student learning.

- **Time to plan with general education colleagues**. Teachers from general education and special education are held accountable for increasing the performance of all students, so it is vital that the special educator be a part of a general education team. General education and special education teachers may plan together and work to ensure that all students have access to the curriculum. For inclusive classrooms to be successful, planning between general and special educators must be a top priority. The team must communicate, collaborate, and plan to meet the needs of children with disabilities. This is a positive step toward the goal of improved instruction and increased performance for all students.

- **Time to reflect**. Beginning and veteran teachers benefit by becoming reflective practitioners. Mentors must be certain to speak in reflective and noncritical ways. This encourages new teachers to review and adapt their teaching strategies, revise future lessons, and incorporate new information into their practice (Scherer, 1999). Incorporating the technique of reflection into their practice encourages continued participation in the learning community for both the mentor and new teacher. It may be helpful for the beginning teacher to keep a journal of these reflections. This process will require time for both teachers to give thoughtful consideration to their reflections.

- **Time to observe**. It is not only essential for the mentor and mentee to spend time together, but the beginning teacher also will benefit by observing a variety of teaching styles in different classrooms. The beginning teacher can reflect on these observations and determine which strategies may be worth incorporating into his or her own repertoire. He or she may wish to explore these options with the mentor teacher.

When educators have the time to plan, communicate, and collaborate, students in special education can achieve high and challenging standards. For the mentor and new teacher, shared experience has a more powerful impact than conversations and planning alone; therefore it is vital that the teachers have time to spend observing in each others' classrooms. Principals should keep this in mind when scheduling for the beginning teacher.

Creative Scheduling

Mentoring is found to be most effective when the beginning teacher and the mentor plan together at least once a week (Whitaker, 2000). This may involve creative scheduling—including scheduling concurrent planning times or lunches. Principals also may want to release the mentor and mentee from school-related duties, such as bus duty, to make meeting more convenient. Several strategies for expanding time for mentoring include:

- Ask staff to identify with whom and when they need to collaborate, and redesign the master schedule to accommodate these needs.

- Hire permanent substitutes to rotate through classrooms to periodically free up teachers to attend meetings during the day rather than before or after school.

- Institute a community service component to the curriculum. When students are in the

community (e.g., Thursday afternoon) teachers meet.

- Schedule specials (e.g., art, music, etc.), clubs, and tutorials during the same time blocks (e.g., first and second period), so teachers have one or two hours a day to collaborate.

- Engage parent and community members to plan and conduct half-day or full-day exploratory, craft, hobby (e.g., gourmet cooking, puppetry, photography), theater, or other experiential programs.

- Partner with colleges and universities. Have their faculty teach lessons, provide demonstrations, or offer on-campus experiences to free up school personnel.

- Earmark some staff development days for collaborative meetings.

- Use faculty meeting time for small-group meetings to solve problems related to issues of immediate and long-range importance.

- Rearrange the school day to include a 50- to 60-minute block of time before or after school for collaborative meeting and planning.

- Build into the school schedule at least one collaboration day per marking period or month.

■ *School-Related Information*

The area of providing the beginning teacher with information regarding the school—such as policies, procedures, and forms—is sometimes overlooked (Whitaker, 2000). Principals will want to provide a school handbook and ask the mentor to assist the beginning teacher in navigating the necessary forms and documentation (Hillebrand, 1999).

Help with Paperwork

The amount of paperwork required of special educators is one of their most serious concerns (Kozleski et al., 2001). It can derail the new teacher's ability to deliver high-quality services and will, therefore, impact student performance. Beginning teachers need assistance with paperwork that is specific to their district, such as discipline forms, documentation of skill attainment, or parent letters.

A mentor who reviews paperwork with the beginning teacher provides valuable guidance concerning the proper procedures within that district. The importance of this help was expressed best by a beginning teacher who asked for help in figuring out how to deal with paperwork. She wanted someone to provide support and feedback to her when she wrote her first IEP (Hillebrand, 1999).

Resource People

Beginning teachers need to familiarize themselves with the resources in their district. They need to be introduced to the special education administrator if one is assigned, as well as to specialists who can help meet the needs of their students. The physical therapist may assist in securing necessary equipment for a child with physical disabilities, for example, and the speech/language pathologist may assist with technology equipment for a child with a communication disorder. Manuals and curriculum guides for general educators also should be made available to special educators.

Classroom Assignment

Another way to support the beginning teacher as part of the school team is to locate the classroom appropriately. The special education classroom should be assigned a room in the mainstream of the school. This allows the teachers the opportunity to be accessible for collaboration with general educators and reduces the walk back and forth for the students when changing classes. The building should be accessible to children with all types of disabilities.

Reasonable Caseloads

Special educators identify their burgeoning caseloads as a critical concern (Kozleski et al., 2001). There also is an increased demand for collaboration with caregivers and general educators. When determining the beginning special educator's caseload, consider the learning needs of the students, the array of responsibil-

ities assigned to the teacher, and the resources available (Kozleski et al., 2001). Principals must take special care not to overburden the beginning teacher with an overly demanding caseload.

Working with Paraprofessionals

Beginning teachers often have little training or experience in supervising paraprofessionals, so it is vital to assign an appropriate paraprofessional to work with them. The paraprofessional should be someone who has some training in working with children with disabilities. Expectations for the paraprofessional should be clearly defined, and the teacher should be provided with the job description so that he or she is aware of those expectations.

■ *Professional Development*

It is vital that the beginning special educator develop skills for collaboration. The collaboration of general and special educators may take one or more forms. The teachers may co-teach across subject areas in either large or small groups. The special education teacher may be a part of the school support team and/or a consultant in a classroom.

The principal and the mentor teacher can work with the beginning teacher to develop collaboration skills through individual meetings or districtwide staff development activities. (The mentoring coordinator can provide information about the availability of these sessions). The principal can support collaboration through several specific actions. These include:

- Supporting collaboration by providing flexible scheduling (Friend, 2001). For example, this can be done by encouraging the use of other adults to help cover classes, including the principal, assistant principal, counselors, social workers, volunteers, paraprofessionals, psychologists, and supervisors—being careful to follow local policies regarding who can supervise groups of students.

- Assisting in arranging for and funding substitutes. The principal may be able to allocate funds from state or local foundations, parent-teacher organizations, and disability advocacy groups.

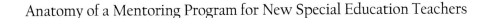

To locate substitutes, the principal can reach out to diverse groups who may consider substituting (e.g., retired teachers, members of social or civic organizations, and teacher trainees from local universities). The mentoring coordinator may have already made these arrangements or may be able to assist in making them.

- Experimenting with a late arrival or early dismissal day. Typically, a principal can lengthen the school day and bank the additional minutes to provide the release time for the beginning teacher to work with colleagues.

- Encouraging teachers to divide labor to save time. For example, the principal can encourage

☐ The Role of the Principal in Supporting First-Year Special Education Teachers

Ways to Support the New Teacher in the Classroom

- Visit the beginning teacher's classroom.

- Review the beginning teacher's lesson plans.

- Provide positive feedback.

- Keep an open-door policy so that the beginning teacher is comfortable talking with you.

- Be available to assist the beginning teacher with difficult parents.

- Participate in IEP meetings for the beginning teacher's students.

- Provide opportunities for the new teacher to observe other teachers with a variety of teaching styles.

Ways to Support the New Teacher in the School Community

- Stress how valuable the beginning teacher is to the school when introducing him or her to the staff.

- Make resources from the general education and special education curriculum available to the beginning teacher.

- Reduce outside requirements, such as committees and extracurricular activities,

so that the beginning teacher can focus on teaching.

- Make the classroom accessible and in the mainstream of the school.

- Be sure the paraprofessional has the necessary training.

Ways to Support the Mentoring Relationship

- Collaborate with the mentoring coordinator.

- Make sure the mentor-mentee match is a good one.

- Follow up on incentives for mentors (e.g., CEUs, compensation time, stipends, or graduate credit).

- Provide time for the mentor and new teachers to meet (e.g., conference, reflect, problem solve, plan strategies, observe each other's teaching, etc.).

- Make schedules so that the mentor and new teacher have concurrent lunch or planning times, or are relieved from extra duties (such as bus duty).

- Pursue professional development opportunities for the mentor and new teacher to participate in together.

one teacher to take the lead in preparing materials for different lessons, making enough copies for all involved.

- Reserving time in special educators' daily schedules that is not obligated to specific responsibilities so they can meet with general educators.

Special Education Concerns

When planning professional development activities, principals can benefit from talking with special educators about their specific development needs. Principals should check with the mentor coordinator on the assessments that will be used with the mentoring program in the district.

Beginning special educators should be encouraged to participate in professional development activities. They will need content-oriented and skill-oriented professional development similar to that needed by general educators (Bateman & Bateman, 2006). When planning professional development activities, the principal must ensure that all staff are knowledgeable about the IDEA requirements and demonstrate effective practices for working with children with disabilities. This will ease the way for the beginning teacher in collaborating and planning with general educators.

Shared Development Opportunities

To build a sense of teaming and collaboration, the principal must ensure that the general educator, the special educator, and the paraprofessional have the opportunity to attend professional development activities together. This also will enable the team members to work in a cooperative and collaborative manner when planning strategies for instruction. The sense of work-

ing together fostered by this environment is in the best interest of all children.

"Administration wise, I feel a lot of support. I know that they're always there."

—**New Teacher Mentoring Induction Project**

Funds for Materials

Funds must be made available for the beginning special educator to order necessary materials (Whitaker, 2000). Purchase orders may have been turned in prior to the beginning teacher being hired. If so, the principal should ensure that the beginning teacher has the opportunity to order necessary materials specific to his or her personal teaching style.

Contact with Program Coordinators

The principal is the contact person for the mentor induction program coordinators and will need to keep them informed of the work with the new teachers. The principal must maintain confidentiality in these exchanges (Fideler & Haselkorn, 1999). Principals should share any recommendations for further professional development with the program coordinators.

In conclusion, the principal is the key to the success of first-year special educators. A supportive induction team—consisting of the principal, the beginning teacher, and the mentor—will help the beginning teacher grow professionally and may also encourage him or her to remain in the field of teaching.

Epilogue

As this book is set to go to press, we find that many issues surrounding the qualifications, certification, and retention of special educators are coming to the forefront. Districts and states are wrestling with the definitions of "highly qualified" and the implications of these shifts for special educators in varying roles and positions. This is happening even as those in special education continue to voice all of the many reasons for special educators to be considered "highly qualified" in their own right.

Why should a special educator at the secondary level only be considered highly qualified if he or she has majored in and/or passed a test in an academic subject area? Why can't a resource teacher be considered highly qualified based on the myriad skills and his or her knowledge regarding how to reach and teach students who are at the margins? The good news is that many groups—including the National Governor's Association—are beginning to look at these issues. There is some confidence that modifications to NCLB in relationship to special education will be forthcoming.

At the same time that the concept of highly qualified continues to be debated, growing numbers of teachers—in both general and special education—are becoming certified through alternative routes (Feistritzer, 2005). Even with this influx of teachers, however, shortages continue to exist. Other recent data suggest that it is not so much a shortage of teachers as it is a mis-distribution, with high needs in rural and urban areas and in specific areas (math, science, special education, and English as a Second Language). Perhaps, if this is the case, there is some option for convincing existing teachers to become certified in high-need fields such as special education.

How does mentoring for special educators fit into this national picture? In particular, what needs to happen with mentoring of new special education teachers? Following are some thoughts on the subject:

- Mentoring for special educators continues to be desired and effective, and studies continue to support the value of such programs and the positive impact, particularly on teacher retention.

- Research continues to indicate that quality mentoring—that is, mentoring that meets basic criteria in terms of the preparation of the mentor, the support of building administrators, and adequate release time for observation and conferencing—produces better results than mentoring that does not include these provisions. This holds true for teachers across subject areas and grade levels.

- Mentoring combined with adjustment to teaching loads for new teachers, supports such as teacher aides, assistance from an external organization, a supportive principal, a pleasant work environment, and quality professional development activities is more effective than mentoring by itself.

- Mentoring is being used widely with teachers in alternative certification programs, yet little research has been conducted to verify the most effective mentoring for these teachers, who are trained on the job as they teach.

- Adequate induction supports prior to the beginning of the academic school year are essential.

We also know that—just as in real estate—location makes a difference. Teaching in a high poverty school increases the risk of leaving by as much as 50 percent (Johnson et al., 2004).

In a large-scale review of new teachers conducted by reviewing the National Center for Education Statistics database, Smith and Ingersoll (2004) found that 41 percent of new teachers said working with a mentor was very helpful. Another 28 percent said it was somewhat helpful. A quarter of new teachers reported that they worked with mentors several times a week, and another 23 percent indicated that they worked with their mentor at least one time a week. In comparison, support of a principal was viewed as less frequent and less meaningful. Twenty percent of new teachers reported that they received support from their principals a few times a year.

So, in light of these trends and the scarcity of some data, what recommendations can be made to those implementing mentoring?

- Budget for and ensure adequate resources and support.

- Structure mentoring so that special educators collaborate with general educators in planning, implementing, and evaluating your mentoring program.

- Realize that the mentoring guidelines and checklists in this manual continue to be on track. Strong teams of new teachers, mentors, and administrators are needed—with adequate supports and positive working conditions—to ensure that mentoring is effective.

And finally, with the press for AYP, how a mentor operates, including how directive a mentor is, may need to be reevaluated. Under the current reform agenda, the pressures are such that mentoring practices may need to evolve to keep pace with the needs of new teachers.

References

Akron Public Schools. (2002). Various unpublished documents (district mentoring program). Akron, OH: Akron Public Schools Staff Development Center.

American Association for Employment in Education. (1999). *Recruiter's guide: Job fairs for educators.* Columbus, OH: Author.

American Federation of Teachers. (2001). *Beginning teacher induction: The essential bridge.* (Policy Brief No. 13). Washington, DC: Author.

Auton, S., Berry, D., Mullen, S., & Cochran, R. (2002). Induction program for beginners benefit veteran teachers, too. *Journal of Staff Development, 23*(4). Retrieved on March 15, 2007, from **http://www.nsdc.org/library/publications/jsd/auton234.pdf**.

Bartholomay, T., Wallace, T., & Mason, C. (2001). *The leadership factor: A key to effective inclusive high schools.* Minneapolis, MN: University of Minnesota.

Bateman, D., & Bateman, F. (2006). *A principal's guide to special education.* Arlington, VA: Council for Exceptional Children.

Billingsley, B. S. (1993). Teacher retention and attrition in special and general education: A critical review of the literature. *Journal of Special Education, 27*(1), 137-174.

Billingsley, B. S. (2002). *Special education teacher retention and attrition: A critical analysis of the literature.* Washington, DC: Author.

Billingsley, B., Carlson, E., & Klein, S. (2004). The working conditions and induction support of early career special educators. *Exceptional Children, 70*(3), 333-347.

Billingsley, B. S. & Cross, L. H. (1991). Teacher's decision to transfer from special to general education. *Journal of Special Education, 24,* 496-511

Billingsley, B. S., & Tomchin, E. M. (1992). Four beginning LD teachers: What their experiences suggest for trainers and employers. *Learning Disabilities Research and Practice, 7,* 104-112.

Black, S. (2001). A lifeboat for new teachers. *American School Board Journal, 188*(9), 1-5.

Bliss, W. (2000). The business forecast and impact of employee turnover. *Electronic Recruiting Forum.* Retrieved on January 2, 2003, from **http://www.hrfocus.com/forum**.

Boe, E. E., Barkanic, G., & Lowe, C. S. (1999). *Retention and attrition of teachers at the school level: National trends and predictors.* Philadelphia, PA: Center for Research and Evaluation in Social Policy.

Boe, E. E., Bobbitt, S. A., Cook, L. H., & Barkanic, G. (1998). *National trends in teacher supply and turnover for special and general education* (ERIC Document Reproduction Service No. ED 426549). Philadelphia, PA: Center for Research and Evaluation in Social Policy.

Boyer, L. (1999). *A qualitative analysis of the impact of mentorships on new special educator's decisions to remain in the field of special education.* Unpublished doctoral dissertation. George Mason University, Fairfax, VA.

Boyer, L., & Gillespie, P. (2000). Keeping the committed: The importance of induction and support programs for new special educators. *TEACHING Exceptional Children, 33*(1), 10-15.

Boyer, L., & Lee, C. (2001). Converting challenge to success: Supporting a new teacher of students with autism. *Journal of Special Education, 35,* 75-83.

Brock, B. L., & Grady, M. (1998). Beginning teacher induction programs: The role of the principal. *Clearing House, 71,* 179-183.

Brownell, M. T., & Smith, S. W. (1993). Understanding special education teacher attrition: A conceptual model and implications for teacher educators. *Teacher Education and Special Education, 16,* 270-282.

Brownell , M., Yeager, E. A., Sindelar, P., Van Hoover, S., & Riley, T. (2004). Teacher learning cohorts: A vehicle for supporting beginning teachers. *Teacher Education and Special Education, 27*(2), 174-189.

Carter, K. B., & Scruggs, T. E. (2001). Thirty-one students: Reflections of a first-year teacher of students with mental retardation. *Journal of Special Education, 35,*100-104.

Center on Personnel Studies in Special Education (2004). *Workforce watch: An insufficient supply and growing demand for qualified special education teachers.* Retrieved July 6, 2005, from **http://www.copsse.org**.

Colbert, J. A., & Wolff, D. E. (1992). Surviving in urban schools: A collaborative model for a beginning teacher support system. *Journal of Teacher Education, 43*(3), 193-200.

Council for Exceptional Children. (1997). CEC guidelines for developing a mentorship program for beginning special education teachers. *TEACHING Exceptional Children, 29*(6), 19-21.

Council for Exceptional Children. (2003). *What every special educator must know: The standards for the preparation and licensure of special educators* (5th ed.). Reston, VA: Author.

Council of Administrators of Special Education. (2004). *CASE discussion on best practices on highly qualified and CASE position statement on highly qualified.* Retrieved May 20, 2005, from **http://www.casecec.org/pdf/position/Highly%20Qualified%204-14-04.pdf**.

Cross, L. H., & Billingsley, B. S. (1994). Testing a model of special education teachers' intentions to stay in teaching. *Exceptional Children, 60*(5), 411-421.

Darling-Hammond, L. (1996). What matters most: A competent teacher for every child. *Phi Delta Kappan, 78*(3), 193-201.

Darling-Hammond, L. (2000). Foreword. In L. Darling-Hammond (Ed.), *Studies of excellence in teacher education: Preparation in the undergraduate years.* Washington, DC: American Association of Colleges for Teacher Education.

Darling-Hammond, L. (2001). The challenge of staffing our schools. *Educational Leadership, 58*(8), 12-17.

Davis, Jr., O. L. (2001). A view of authentic mentorship. *Journal of Curriculum and Supervision, 17,* 1-4.

Denmark, V., & Podsen, I. (2000) The mettle of a mentor. *Journal of Staff Development, 21*(4), 19-22.

District of Columbia Center for Student Support Services. (2006). *Reflective teaching—after the lesson on reflection.* Washington, DC: Author.

Education Week (2004, January 8). *Count me in: Special education in the era of standards, "Highly Qualified?"* Retrieved January 8, 2004, from **http://counts.edweek.org/sreports/QC04/article.cfm?slug=17teachers.h23**.

Ettorre, B. (1997). Employee retention: Keeping the cream. *HR Focus, 74*, 1-3.

Evertson, C. M., & Smithey, M. W. (2000). Mentoring effects on protégés' classroom practice: An experimental field study. *Journal of Educational Research, 93*(5), 294-304.

Feiman-Nemser, S. (1992). *Helping novices learn to teach: Lessons from an experienced support teacher*. East Lansing, MI: National Center for Research on Teacher Learning, Michigan State University.

Feiman-Nemser, S., Carver, C., Schwille, S., & Yusko, B. (2000). Beyond support: Taking new teachers seriously as learners. In M. Scherer (Ed.), *A better beginning: Supporting and mentoring new teachers*. Alexandria, VA: Association for Supervision and Curriculum Development.

Feiman-Nemser, S., & Parker, M. B. (1993). Mentoring in context: A comparison of two U.S. programs for beginning teachers. *International Journal of Educational Research, 19*, 699-718.

Feiman-Nemser, S., Parker, M. B., & Zeichner, K. (1992). *Are mentor teachers teacher educators?* Retrieved on March 15, 2007, from **http://ncrtl.msu.edu/http/rreports/html/pdf/rr9211.pdf**.

Feistritzer, C. (2005). *Profile of alternate route teachers*. Retrieved December 28, 2006, from **http://www.teach-now.org**.

Fideler, E., & Haselkorn, D. (1999). *Learning the ropes: Urban teacher induction programs and practices in the United States*. Belmont, MA: Recruiting New Teachers, Inc.

Fitzenz, J. (1997). It's costly to lose good employees. *Workforce, 76*, 50-51.

Friend, M. (2001). *From concept to reality: strategies for collaboration*. Boston, MA: Allyn & Bacon.

Ganser, T., Bainer, D. L., Bendixem-Noe, M., Brock, B. L., Stinson, A. D., Giebelhaus, C., & Runyon, C. K. (1998). *Critical issues in mentoring and mentoring programs for beginning teachers* (ERIC Document Reproduction Services No. ED 425146).

Gersten, R., Keating, T., Yovanoff, P., & Harniss, M. (2001). Working in special education: Factors that enhance special educators' intent to stay. *Exceptional Children, 67*(4), 549-567.

Gold, Y. (1996). Beginning teacher support: Attrition, mentoring, and induction. In J. Sikula, T. J. Buttery, & E. Guyton (Eds.), *Handbook of research on teacher education: A project of the Association of Teacher Education* (2nd ed.) (pp. 548-594). New York: Macmillan.

Griffin, C. C., Winn, J. A., Otis-Wilborn, A., & Kilgore, K. L. (2003). *New teacher induction in special education*. Gainesville, FL: Center on Personnel Studies in Special Education, University of Florida.

Griffin, G. A. (1985). Teacher induction: research issues. *Journal of Teacher Education, 36*(1),42-46.

Hauenstein, P. (1999). Understanding turnover. *Advantage Hiring Newsletter*. Retrieved on January 2, 2003, from **http://www.advantagehiring.com/newsletter/n99Q4_1.html**.

Hillebrand, M. (1999). Friendly faces, support would make special education teachers stick around. *Special Education News*. Retrieved on July 2, 2002, from **http://www.specialed-news.com/educators/ednews/mentors082899.html**.

Holloway, J. H. (2001). The benefits of mentoring. *Educational Leadership, 58*, 1-4.

Hope, W. C. (1999). Principals' orientation and induction activities as factors. *Clearing House, 73*, 53-55.

Houston, W. R., McDavid, T., & Marshall, F. (1990). A study of the induction of 300 first-year teachers and their mentors, 1989-1990 (ERIC Document Reproduction Service No. 338558).

Huling-Austin, L. (1992). Research on learning to teach: Implications for teacher induction and mentoring programs. *Journal of Teacher Education, 43*(3), 173-180.

Illinois State Board of Education. (October, 2000). *Work study session I and plenary business meeting*. Retrieved December 6, 2002, from **http://www.isbe.net/board/meetings/junemeeting**.

Johnson, S. M., & Kardos, S. M. (2002). Keeping new teachers in mind. *Educational Leadership, 59*(6), 12-16.

Johnson, S., Kardos, M., Kauffman, D., Liu, E., & Donaldson, M. (2004). The support gap: New teachers' early experiences in high-income and low-income schools. Paper presented at the 2004 Annual Meeting of the American Educational Research Association, San Diego, CA.

King-Sears, M. E. (1995). Teamwork toward inclusion: A school system and university partnership for practicing educators. *Action in Teacher Education, 17*(3), 54-66.

Kozelski, E., Mainzer, R., & Deschler, D. (2001). *Bright futures for exceptional learners: An action agenda to achieve quality conditions for teaching and learning*. Arlington, VA: Council for Exceptional Children.

Lane, G. M., & Canosa, R. (1995). A mentoring program for beginning and veteran teachers of students with severe disabilities. *Teacher Education and Special Education, 18*(4), 230-239.

Lawson, H. A. (1992). Beyond the new conception of teacher induction. *Journal of Teacher Education, 43*(3), 163-172.

Learning Point Associates. (2004). *Recruitment and retention: State policy.* Retrieved July 13, 2005, from **http://www.tqsource.org/randr/policy/index.asp**.

Little, J. W. (1990). The mentor phenomenon and the social organization of teaching. *Review of Research in Education, 16*, 297-351.

Mason, C. (2006). *Transition to teaching.* Washington, DC: Student Support Center, District of Columbia Public Schools.

Mason, C., & O'Connell, M. (2002). *Costs and cost effectiveness of operating mentoring induction programs in special education.* Unpublished data.

Mason, C., & White, M. (2003). *Guide for mentoring special education teachers.* Arlington, VA: Council for Exceptional Children.

Mastropieri, M. A. (2001). Introduction to the special issue: Is the glass half full or half empty? Challenges encountered by first-year special education teachers. *Journal of Special Education, 35*(2), 66-74.

Miles, K. H., Odden, A., Fermanich, M., Archibald, S., & Gallagher, A. (2002). An analysis of professional development spending in four districts using a new cost framework. Madison, WI: Consortium for Policy Research in Education, University of Wisconsin-Madison.

Miller, M. D, Brownell, M. T., & Smith, S. W. (1999). Factors that predict teachers staying and leaving, or transferring from the special education classroom. *Exceptional Children, 65*(2), 201-218.

Miller, B., Lord, B., & Dorney, J. (1994). *Staff development for teachers: A study of configurations and costs in four districts.* Newton, MA: Education Development Center.

North Carolina State Department of Public Instruction. (1997). *Toolkit for mentoring.* Raleigh, NC: Author.

Odell, S. J., & Ferraro, D. P. (1992). Teacher mentoring and teacher retention. *Journal of Teacher Education, 43*(3), 200-204.

Office of Special Education Programs. (2002). *Twenty-third annual report to Congress on the implementation of the Individuals with disabilities Education Act.* Washington, DC: U.S. Department of Education.

Oregon Recruitment and Retention Project. (2004). *Results from a recently conducted survey of newly hired special education professionals in Oregon.* Monmouth, OR: Teaching Research Division, Western Oregon University.

Peterson, R. (2002). *How to organize and evaluate a mentor program: Mentor teacher's handbook.* Irvine, CA: University of California.

Portner, H. (1999). *Mentoring new teachers.* Thousand Oaks, CA: Corwin Press.

Recruiting New Teachers. (1999). *Learning the ropes: Urban teacher induction programs and practices in the United States.* Retrieved on February 13, 2003, from **http://www.rnt.org/publications/ropes.html**.

Rowley, J. B. (1999). The good mentor. *Educational Leadership, 56*(8), 20-22.

Scherer, M. (1999). *A better beginning: Supporting and mentoring new teachers.* Alexandria, VA: Association for Supervision and Curriculum Development.

Singh, K., & Billingsley, B. S. (1996). Intent to stay in teaching: Teachers of students with emotional disorders versus other special educators. *Remedial and Special Education, 17*(1), 37-47.

Smith, T. M., & Ingersoll, R. M. (2004). What are the effects of induction and mentoring on beginning teacher turnover? *American Educational Research Journal, 41*(3), 681–714.

Study of Personnel Needs in Special Education. (2001). *Service provider survey: School climate instrument.* Retrieved on February 23, 2003, from **www.spense.org**.

Tindle, D. (2006). Mentoring new teachers. In C. Mason, M. Thormann, F. Harris-Burke, & J. Burnette (Eds.), *Mentoring new teachers.* Washington, DC: Center for Student Support Services.

Urban Teacher Collaborative. (2000). *The urban teacher challenge: Teacher demand and supply in the great city schools.* Belmont, MA: Recruiting New Teachers.

U.S. Department of Education. (2004). *Improving teacher quality state grants: Non-regulatory guidance.* Retrieved on July 7, 2005, from **http://www.ed.gov/programs/teacherqual/guidance.doc**.

Villani, S. (2002). *Mentoring programs for new teachers: Models of induction and support*. Thousands Oaks, CA: Corwin Press.

Wald, J. L. (1998). *Retention of special education professionals: A practical guide of strategies and activities for educators and administrators*. Arlington, VA: National Clearinghouse for Professions in Special Education, Council for Exceptional Children.

Wang, J., & Odell, S. J. (2002). Learning to teach according to standards-based reform: A critical review. *Review of Educational Research, 72*(3), 481-546.

Wanzare, Z., & da Costa, J. L. (2000) Supervision and staff development: Overview of the literature. *NASSP Bulletin, 84*(618), 47-54.

Westling, D. L., & Whitten, T. M. (1996). Rural special education teachers' plans to continue or leave their teaching positions. *Exceptional Children, 62*(4), 319-35.

Whitaker, S. D. (2000). Supporting beginning special education teachers. *Focus on Exceptional Children, 34*,1-18.

White, M. (1995). *Factors contributing to special education teacher attrition: How a one year internship affects the attrition rates of special education teachers in Kentucky*. Unpublished doctoral dissertation, Vanderbilt University, Nashville, TN.

White, M., & Mason, C. (2002). *Data Set from the Mentoring Induction Project*. Unpublished data.

White, M., & Mason, C. Y. (2006). Components of a successful mentoring program for beginning special education teachers: Perspectives from new teachers and mentors. *Teacher Education and Special Education, 29*(3), pp. 191-201.

Whisnant, E., Elliott, K., & Pynchon, S. (2005). *A review of literature on beginning teacher induction*. Retrieved December 28, 2006, from **http://www.cst-pwa.org/Navigational/Policies_practices/Teacher_induction/A_Review_of_Literature.pdf**.

Wong, H., & Wong, R. (2002). *Effective teaching*. Retrieved on December 6, 2002, from **http://teachers.net/gazette/MAY02?wong.html**.